Human Biology

Human Biology

Michael Gabb, BSc

HUTCHINSON EDUCATIONAL

HUTCHINSON EDUCATIONAL LTD
3 Fitzroy Square, London W1

London Melbourne Sydney Auckland Wellington Johannesburg Cape Town and agencies throughout the world

First published 1974

Text © Michael Gabb 1974
Illustrations © Hutchinson Educational Ltd 1974

Printed and bound in Great Britain by
REDWOOD BURN LIMITED
Trowbridge & Esher

ISBN 0 09 112341 0

Contents

Preface	vii
1 Introducing Man	8
What is a human being	8
The body's inner machinery	11
2 Food, feeding and digestion	12
What is a healthy diet	12
Carbohydrates, fats and proteins	13
The quality of food	13
The main vitamins required by man	14
Diet around the world	15
Identifying food substances	17
Practical Exercises	17
Teeth	18
Digestion	20
Practical work on hydrolysis	20
A summary of digestion	20
Absorption	23
The Liver	23
Producing enough food	24
Preserving foods	26
3 Breathing and respiration	31
The breathing system	31
The mechanics of breathing	32
Air exchange in breathing	32
The composition of inspired and expired air	33
The human breathing system—its structure	33
Recording breathing movements	35
Respiration	36
The blood and breathing	37
The rhesus factor	38
4 The heart and circulation	39
Measurement of pulse rate	40
The structure of the heart	42
The blood vessels	44
The body fluids	46
The lymphatic system	48
5 Excretion: the removal of waste	49
The work of the kidneys	49
The structure of the kidneys	50
6 The skin and heat loss	53
The skin: its structure and function	53
7 The skeleton and muscles	56
The role of the skeleton	56
The structure of the skeleton	58
Bones as levers	59

The construction of bones	59
Muscles and their action	60
The types of muscles	61

8 The body's control systems — 62

The nervous system	64
The reflex arc	65
Chemical messengers	65
Hormones	66
Insulin: its discovery and development	69
The senses	70
The skin	70
Taste and smell	71
The eye and sight	72
The ear: organ of hearing and balance	73
Practical Problems	74

9 Reproduction — 82

The human reproductive system	82
Fertilization	83
Pregnancy	85
Problems	87

10 Cells and genetics — 88

Cells and tissues	88
Cells under the microscope	89
The nucleus	90
Introducing genetics	91
Mendel's experiments	91
Parents and children	94
Boy or girl?	96
Breeding plants and animals	96
Cell reproduction	97
Mitosis	98
Meiosis	99

11 Disease causing organisms — 100

Viruses	100
Practical Problems	101
Bacteria	102
Vaccination and immunity	104
Identifying bacteria	105
Antibiotics	106
Protozoa	107
Worms	108
Mites	109
Fungi	109
Insects	109

12 The community and its services — 110

Controlling epidemic disease	110
The supply of water	112
Refuse collection and disposal	114
Sewage disposal	115
Air pollution	116
Town planning and urban development	117

Preface

A welcome trend in the teaching of biology is the ever-increasing use of an experimental and observational approach in which the pupil is encouraged to think for him— or herself; to make observations on living and dead material, to devise experiments, record results and draw appropriate conclusions. Many teachers have been greatly encouraged, even surprised, by the ingenuity displayed by apparently average or below average pupils, and by the increased level of interest and enjoyment.

An attempt has been made here to introduce sufficient practical work, problem solving material and examples from everyday life to stimulate the student and to encourage him to achieve a worthwhile understanding of what a human being is both anatomically and physiologically and to develop the ability to appreciate what is fact and what is opinion based on available information.

Human Biology is intended to cover the various regional syllabuses leading to the Certificate of Secondary Education, but it should also provide a useful background to the subject for GCE Ordinary level pupils.

M.H.G.

Acknowledgements
I would like to acknowledge the help of a number of individuals and organisations who have helped by providing advice, information, illustrative references and material; in particular to Design Practitioners Limited, Sevenoaks, Kent, for the drawings, Dr Alan Harris, Dr Guido Pincherle, The Genito Urinary Manufacturing Company, Mr Bill Dunn of the United States Information Services and my publishers, especially Mr Philip Kogan and Miss Elaine Hopton.

1 Introducing man

What is a human being?
How do we differ from other animals? Which animals do you think are most like humans and why?

Scientists who study animals, called *zoologists,* arrange or *classify* all the many different kinds of animals into groups by comparing their likenesses and differences. The sort of features that a zoologist looks for are the presence or absence of an inner, bony skeleton with joints, a hard, unjointed outer shell, or a hard jointed outer shell; the presence or absence of wings; whether the skin contains scales, hair or feathers; the structure and arrangement of a nervous system if the animal has one.

The drawings show a range of animals with their skeletal and nervous systems highly simplified; compare them, noting their differences and similarities, and arrange them in groups containing those that are most like each other. List the likenesses that have made you place the animals in each group.

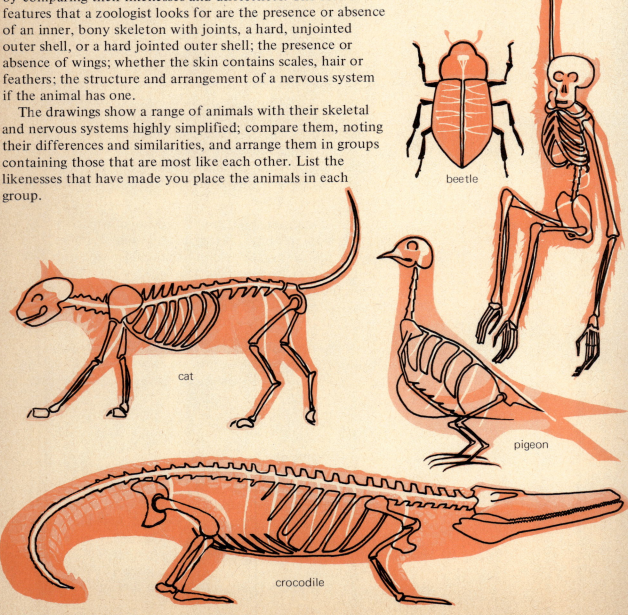

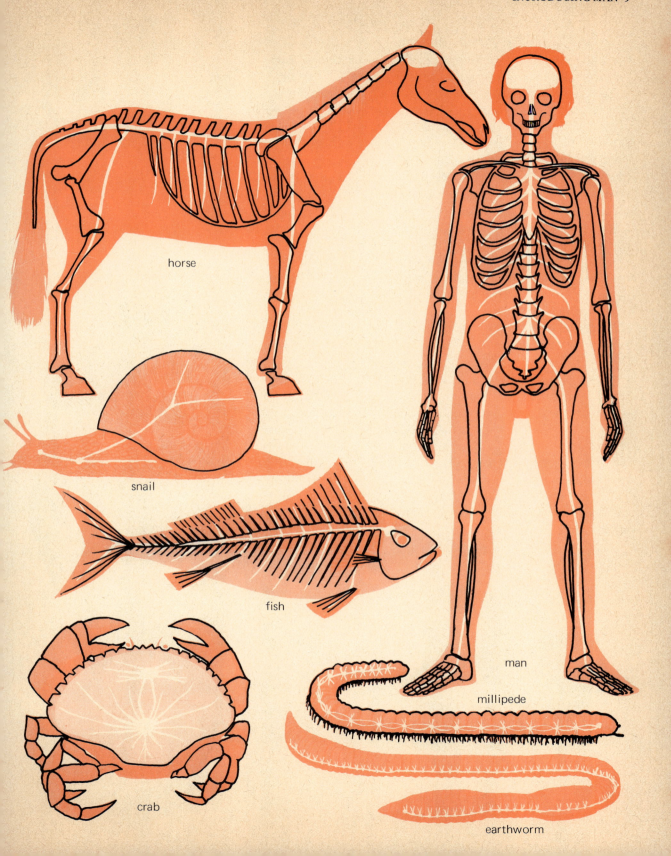

All the animals in a major group will have a few basic features in common, but within this group some animals will be more alike than others, and these will be placed in subgroups. This process is repeated until each type of animal can be placed in a group called *genus* within which are collected the smallest groups of all called *species*. Each animal is given the name of its genus (the generic name) and a species (or *specific* name). All humans, for instance, are named *Homo sapiens.* (Latin names are always used so that in any country a standard method of naming is followed and any scientist knows without possible confusion which animal is referred to. Common names for animals often refer to completely different animals in another country).

Other species are grouped with man in genus *Homo* but only ones now extinct. One near relative is Neanderthal man, *Homo neanderthalensis,* who lived 50,000 years ago. Some other extinct man-like creatures are considered sufficiently different to be placed in different genera, but all are sufficiently man-like to be included in the same family, the *Hominidae.*

Man's closest living animal relatives are the apes, including the gorilla, the orang-utan, the chimpanzee and the gibbons. If you have ever looked closely at any of these animals in the zoo you cannot fail to be impressed by the similarities between them and humans. But there are also many differences, not least the great size and development of the brain in humans and the upright walk. In the chapters that follow we shall be looking at the features of man's structure (*anatomy*) and the workings of man's body (its *physiology*) which make us unique in the animal kingdom.

chimpanzee

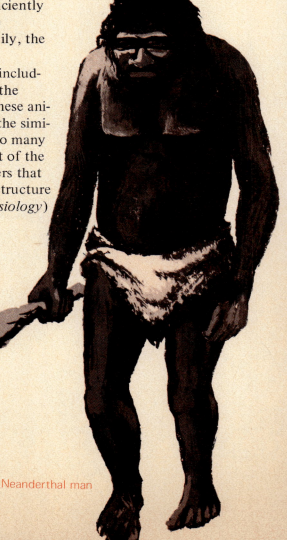
Neanderthal man

The body's inner machinery

A car engine is a precisely made piece of machinery. Its parts are made and assembled accurately. To help them move against each other the engine is supplied with lubricating oil, and in order to work it must be fed with petrol and air. Worn and damaged parts have to be replaced when necessary. If you want to find out what the various parts of a car engine are and what they do you have to take it to pieces. You can then see how each part is connected to the others and discover how the materials pass into and out of the engine and what each part does.

The human body requires food, oxygen and water. What happens to these substances inside the body? Food passes into the mouth; where does it pass afterwards and how is it made use of? Is any of it discarded and how are the unwanted parts got rid of? We breathe in air; what happens to it? Does the composition of the air we breathe in differ from the air we breathe out? The car engine produces exhaust gases which are removed through the exhaust system. The body produces waste materials; how are these removed? Why is it necessary to remove them?

Clearly there are many more such questions that we could ask. It is the physiologist's job to try to answer them. In looking at the discoveries that have been made and by performing simple investigations it is possible to provide answers to many of them.

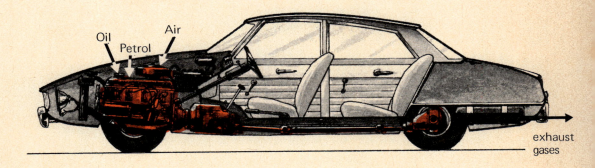

'A car uses petrol and air and electricity to provide energy to move—it passes gases out of the exhaust—and the parts must be well lubricated and kept in good order for it to be an efficient piece of machinery'

2 Food, feeding and digestion

A car engine needs fuel in order to work. When the fuel is burnt it releases energy in an explosion which pushes against the pistons and forces them to move. This in turn causes other moveable parts connected to the pistons to move. Waste gases are formed in the explosion and have to be removed through the exhaust system. Periodically the parts wear out and have to be repaired or replaced.

Similarly, humans, like other animals, require energy for muscles to work, for repair of worn or damaged tissues, for growth, for combating infections and for other living processes. In women, particularly heavy demands for energy are made during pregnancy and breast feeding. The energy required for living processes is obtained from foods.

Many of the food molecules are complicated and have to be split into simpler ones before the body can utilize them. This is achieved during *digestion* by the action of *enzymes*. If the body is to remain healthy certain kinds of foods must be taken in sufficient quantities and at reasonably regular intervals.

What is a healthy diet?
The food substances essential to health include *carbohydrates, fats, proteins,* some *minerals, vitamins*—in minute quantities—and *water*. Most of the energy that the body requires is obtained from carbohydrates and fats, but proteins can be burnt to provide energy. (Muscle tissue is mostly composed of protein and in countries such as India, where the average diet is poor, many of the people have wasted bodies due to the burning of their muscle protein to provide energy.)

Minerals are required by the body for a variety of reasons. Bones and teeth consist largely of minerals, which are also important for the proper working of nerves and muscles, and of the blood in carrying oxygen. (Lack of iron, for instance, causes anaemia when the blood is a less efficient carrier of oxygen). Some enzymes necessary for the digestion of food will not work in the absence of certain minerals. The storage and release of energy in the cells of the body is achieved by means of substances containing the mineral phosphorus.

Fig 1.
Daily calorie requirements

FOOD, FEEDING AND DIGESTION

Vitamins are required only in tiny amounts. They are organic compounds whose absence or deficiency from the diet so disrupts the body's normal workings that certain diseases—deficiency diseases—result. For instance, lack of vitamin D_2 produces rickets, a disease affecting the growth of bones and teeth. The main vitamins required by man, the foods in which they occur and the deficiency diseases resulting from their absence are summarised in the table on page 14.

Water is needed mainly because the body's chemical reactions take place in solution; it comprises 70 per cent of the body by weight.

Carbohydrates, fats and proteins

These three kinds of carbon-containing compounds are basic constituents of all but the simplest living things. Carbohydrates contain carbon, hydrogen and oxygen. *Glucose* (grape sugar), *sucrose* (cane sugar), *fructose* (fruit sugar), *starch* and *cellulose* are all examples. In most carbohydrates hydrogen and oxygen are present in the same proportions as in water—two atoms of hydrogen to each oxygen atom. Apart from water, carbohydrates form the largest part of the diet by weight.

Fats also contain carbon, hydrogen and oxygen, but there is less oxygen than in carbohydrates. Because a greater proportion of a fat than of a carbohydrate is combustible material, fat yields more energy when burnt by the body than does an equal amount of carbohydrate. More water will also be formed. Fats are an important and economical way for the body to store energy.

Proteins contain nitrogen as well as carbon, hydrogen and oxygen, and some also contain sulphur or phosphorus. With water, proteins form the basis of *protoplasm*. All known enzymes are proteins and proteins also form the basic structural material of muscle tissue. Some energy is released from protein breakdown and proteins can be converted into carbohydrates, but they are less important sources of energy than fats and carbohydrates.

The quality of food

How much of each of the three main kinds of food substances do we require and which food do we need to eat to obtain them? Foods rich in starch—a carbohydrate—such as bread and potatoes are noticeably absent from slimming diets because when eaten in excess they cause us to become overweight. This does not happen with protein-rich foods.

The energy value of a food is expressed in *Calories* (or

The main vitamins required by man

Vitamin	Food source	Role in the body	Effects of deficiency
A (Axerophthol)	Fish liver oils, butter, milk, margarine, fresh green vegetables	General resistance to infections, especially those affecting *epithelia* (lining and covering tissues); growth of new cells, and formation of eye pigments	Skin dryness; drying of cornea *(xerophthalmia)*; night blindness; poor growth of bones.
B_1 (Thiamine)	Seeds (especially in germ or embryo) of cereals and legumes, yeast, eggs, liver	Carbohydrate metabolism	Beri-beri
B_2 (Riboflavin)	Yeast and meat extracts (e.g. Bovril) wheat bran, milk, green vegetables	Cell metabolism, especially oxidation reactions	Inflammation of tongue
B_5 (Nicotinic acid)	Yeast, wheat germ, fish, cereals, meat	Protein and carbohydrate metabolism; part of certain enzyme systems	*Pellagra* (general weakness, skin inflammation, diarrhoea and nervous disorders)
B_{12} (Cyanocobalamin)	Liver	Formation of red blood cells	*Pernicious anaemia* (a fatal blood disease)
C (Ascorbic acid)	Oranges, grapefruit, lemons, currants, green vegetables	Healing of wounds, resistance to infection	*Scurvy* (disease affecting joints, with bleeding of gums and other parts)
Choline	Soya beans, liver, pancreas	Fat chemistry; making of acetyl choline (a chemical released by nerve endings)	Cirrhosis of liver; nerve function
D (several forms occur eg D_2, D_3)	Fish liver oils, margarine, eggs, liver, butter	Vital for proper absorption of calcium and phosphorus	*Rickets* (poor bone and teeth growth); *osteomalacia* (bone softening)
E (Tocopherols)	Vegetable oils, eggs, green vegetables	Opposes fat oxidation; concerned with growth of embryos and sperms	Loss of fertility; poor development of foetuses
H (Biotin)	Nuts, egg white, milk, liver	Essential for action of certain enzymes	*Dermatitis* (inflammation of skin, loss of appetite, pains in muscles)
K_1 (Phylloquinone)	Spinach, lettuce, pig liver, tomatoes	Blood clotting	Blood clots very slowly; tendency to bleed excessively

There are many other vitamins than those listed here whose role in other animals is known and whose deficiency has known effects. Folic acid is necessary in minute quantities in the human diet. The best food sources are liver, kidney and fresh vegetables.
Vitamin C is destroyed by boiling the food in air. B_1 is destroyed by heat.

kilocalories). A Calorie is defined as the amount of heat required to raise the temperature of one litre of water by one degree centigrade. The average adult requires about 3000 Calories for his daily diet but this will vary considerably depending on a person's age, sex and occupation. Clearly a coal miner will require more energy per day than an office clerk. In times of illness, and during pregnancy and breast feeding, extra demands for energy will be made by the tissues.

The main sources of energy are carbohydrates: one gram of carbohydrate supplies 4.1 Calories if completely burnt. Cereals, potatoes, bread, rice and chocolate are carbohydrate-rich foods. Protein-rich foods include meat, eggs, fish and peanuts. A gram of protein would yield 4.1 Calories if it were burnt completely. One gram of fat supplies 9.3 Calories; butter, lard, margarine, cheese and bacon are rich in fat. Bacon and cheese also contain appreciable amounts of protein whilst milk is an all-purpose food containing fat, protein and carbohydrate, in addition to minerals such as calcium and phosphorus, and most vitamins.

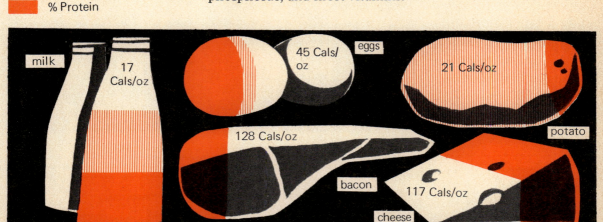

Fig 2. The calorific value of different foods

Diet round the world

Throughout the world there is enormous variation in people's diet, not only in the quantity of food that they eat but also in its quality. Around 70 per cent of the world's population is undernourished. The amount of protein consumed per day is an indication of the diet's quality, as is the proportion of each day's calorie intake derived from carbohydrate. At the present time the most undernourished peoples are those living in southern and eastern Asia. Not only do they have the lowest calorie intake, but a higher proportion of this is derived from carbohydrates than in any other major region. Their protein intake is also the lowest.

It is worth mentioning, however, that in North America and Europe where, as a whole, people eat more food than they actually require, obesity (the condition of being unduly overweight) is common, as are heart diseases, bronchitis and lung cancer. These are the diseases which characterise over-indulgent, overstressed and affluent societies.

Fig 3. Diets around the world

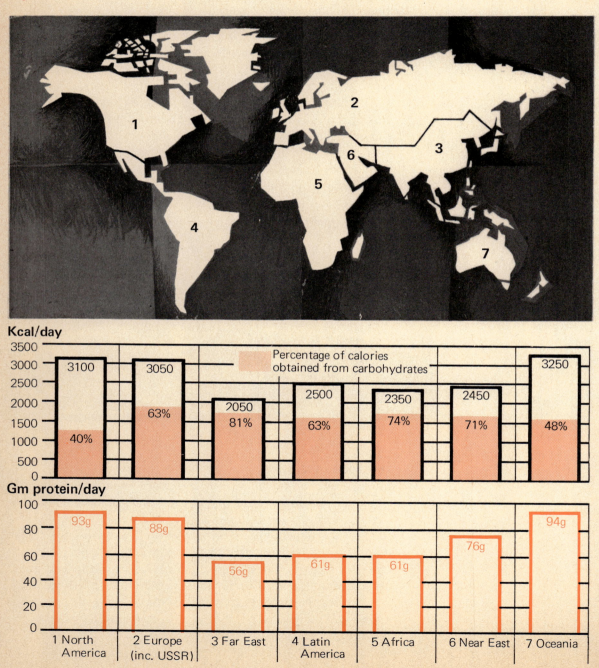

Identifying food substances

Chemical substances can be distinguished by chemical tests. By adding a particular chemical reagent to a food substance it is possible to 'label' it as a carbohydrate, a fat or a protein as the case may be. There are a number of standard tests for identifying these three classes of foods.

Practical work

Apply the following tests in turn to the powders with which your teacher provides you.
Now record your results in table form.
1 *Test with Fehling's solution.* In a boiling tube place a little of the powder to be tested. Add 1 ml Fehling's solution A (copper sulphate) and an equal amount of Fehling's solution B (an alkali mixture). Boil. What happens?
2 *Iodine test.* Add a little iodine solution to each powder in a boiling tube in turn. What do you observe?
3 *Test with carbon tetrachloride.* Add a little carbon tetrachloride to each powder, shaking vigorously, and then place a drop of this mixture on a piece of filter paper. Repeat the test with carbon tetrachloride on its own. Hold the filter paper up to the light and observe.
4 *Test with Millon's reagent.* Add a little Millon's reagent to each powder in turn in a boiling tube, warming the mixture gently. What happens?

The powders could include a protein (e.g. casein from milk), starch, glucose, shredded suet, and malt sugar (maltose). Having performed the four tests on the powders repeat with powdered milk, chalk and cane sugar (sucrose). Repeat the Fehling's test on the chalk and sucrose after first adding hydrochloric acid and boiling. What differences do you observe?

These four tests should also be carried out on foods such as onions, carrots, potatoes, bread, margarine and butter, and the results recorded. The onion, carrot, potato and bread should first be grated and crushed in water and the extracts filtered off before testing.

Olive oil and margarine can also be shaken vigorously in separate test tubes with dilute sodium hydroxide. Repeat with glucose powder. How do the three tubes compare?

Teeth

When we eat food it is broken down into smaller fragments by the crushing, tearing and grinding action of the teeth. A full adult set of teeth numbers thirty-two. If you examine a human skull, complete with its teeth, you will see that the teeth are of a distinctly different shape and size depending on their position in the jaw bones. Those at the front are flat and chisel-like while at the back of the jaw the teeth are much larger with uneven, but not sharp, biting surfaces. The front teeth are the *incisors* used in biting to cut through the food; those at the back are for grinding the food up into smaller pieces.

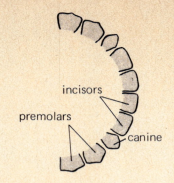

Fig 4. Milk teeth in one jaw

The diagram shows that there are four kinds of teeth in the human jaw, *incisors, canines, premolars,* and *molars.* The number of teeth is expressed in the *dental formula* which indicates how many teeth of each kind are present in one half of each jaw from the incisors in the front to the molars at the back. In humans the dental formula is

$$i2\ c1\ pm\ 2\ m3$$
$$i2\ c1\ pm\ 2\ m3$$

A rabbit has no canine teeth and only one incisor in each half of the lower jaw—its dental formula is

$$2\ 0\ 2\ 3$$
$$1\ 0\ 2\ 3$$

Humans eat all kinds of food—we are *omnivorous*—so our teeth are relatively unspecialised. A rabbit is a plant-eater—it is *herbivorous*—and has a specialised equipment of incisors for cutting its food. The canine teeth, prominent in cats and dogs and used for piercing and tearing flesh, are missing, but the grinding surfaces of the back teeth—molars and premolars— are well developed. In man the canine teeth

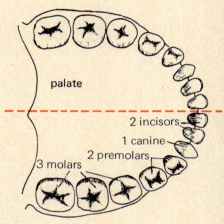

Fig 5. Adult teeth in upper jaw

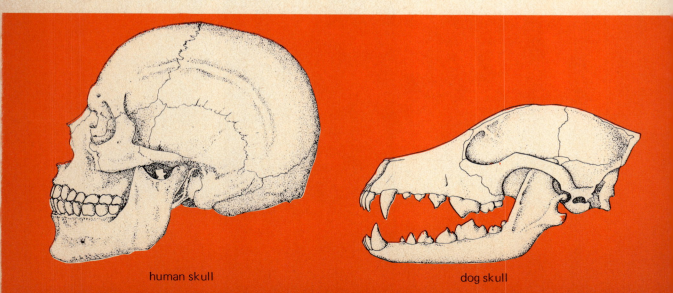

human skull   dog skull

FOOD, FEEDING AND DIGESTION 19

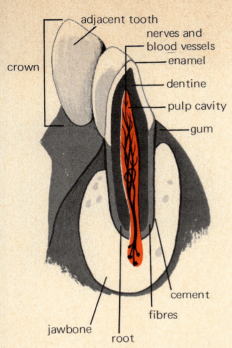

Fig 6. Section through an incisor tooth

Fig 7. Variations in size and shape of animal skulls.
Look at the skulls below. Write down the dental formula for each. What sort of food would you expect each example to eat and why?

are small and work almost as a third incisor.

Although there is a variation in the outward appearance of each type of tooth, structurally all are built to the same basic plan. The diagram shows a vertical section through an incisor tooth. Each tooth is set in a socket in the jawbone; the part below the gum is known as the *root* and the white part above the gum, the *crown.* The bulk of the tooth is composed of a hard bone-like substance called *dentine*; within it is a *pulp cavity*—containing soft, pulpy tissues including blood vessels and nerve fibres. Branches from these pass into the network of fine canals within the dentine. We feel pain when the dentine is damaged by decay or touched by the dentist's drill because the nerve endings within it are stimulated. The crown of the tooth is covered with a hard, white *enamel* and the root by *cementum*—a hard, bone-like substance which holds the tooth firmly in its socket.

Although the adult human has 32 teeth, a child up to the age of about five or six has only 20 teeth. These are called *milk teeth* and are replaced gradually from that age by the second or permanent teeth. The milk teeth consist of incisors, canines, and premolars only; there are no molar teeth. The first milk teeth to appear—usually at about eight or nine months—are the incisors and this set is usually complete soon after the child reaches the age of two. The front molars appear at the age of five or six and they are gradually followed by the rest of the permanent teeth, which grow upwards under the milk teeth. Incisors, premolars and then canines are replaced in that order. At 12 years or so the second molars appear and the wisdom teeth—third molars—usually do not appear until eighteen years or later.

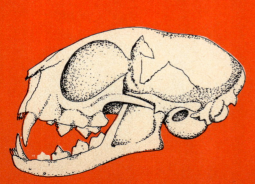

cat skull

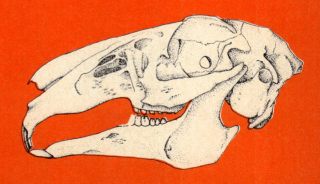

rabbit' skull

Digestion

A healthy diet contains all the food substances that the body requires. As the food passes through the *alimentary canal* a number of changes occur as the body extracts the food substances. These changes start in the mouth where the food is broken down by the action of the jaws and teeth. It is also mixed with saliva produced by the *salivary glands*. This is a watery fluid containing an enzyme, *ptyalin*. Ptyalin acts on starch in the food converting it to maltose, a sugar. An indication of its action can be obtained by placing a little starch on the tongue. It has little or no taste at first but when it has become moistened by the saliva a sweet taste gradually becomes obvious. This is because the starch is being changed into maltose. A chemical change is taking place; the starch is being *hydrolysed* to maltose—hydrolysis literally means water-splitting—in contact with water in the saliva.

Practical work on hydrolysis

1 Add a little soluble starch powder to some water in a boiling tube and boil until the liquid becomes clear
2 Pour a little of the solution into five test tubes
3 Test the solution in one tube for starch with iodine solution (a blue colour indicates starch)
4 To each of the other tubes add one of the following: a little sodium bicarbonate, dilute hydrochloric acid, saliva (collected after first rinsing the mouth to eliminate the possibility of food contaminating it) and boiled saliva
5 On a tile place several drops of iodine
6 Place the four tubes in a water bath at body temperature (36-37°C or about 98°F)
7 At 15-20 second intervals test the liquids in the four tubes with the iodine on the tiles by taking out drops with a pipette. What do you observe in each case? Why is boiled saliva added to one tube? Why is the experiment carried out at body temperature?
8 Test each of the four liquids in the four tubes, after they have been heated for a few minutes by boiling with Fehling's solution. What do you observe?

All the digestive enzymes produced by the digestive glands act through *hydrolysis*. Water (H_2O) is split into two parts, H and OH. The H joins onto one part of the starch 'molecule' which splits away from the main starch structure and OH joins onto the other split part. The end result is the formation of maltose molecules. Note that both the starch and the water are split.

A summary of digestion

Tongue helps to mix food in the mouth.

Teeth break up food into smaller pieces.

Saliva from salivary glands moistens the food. The enzyme *ptyalin* starts to act on starch converting some to maltose, but most of its action takes place in the stomach.

Food passes from mouth into *oesophagus*. Flap of tissue—the *epiglottis*—prevents food from passing down windpipe. Oesophagus has muscular wall which contracts *(peristalsis)* to push food down into *stomach*.

Lining of stomach is rich in gland cells which between them release *hydrochloric acid* which sterilizes the food, the enzyme *pepsin* which starts the breakdown of proteins to *peptones*, the enzyme *rennin* (important in very young children on a milk diet) which clots milk protein *(casein)*. A *lipase* is also present (lipases act on fats). The stomach acts as a mixer of the food and as a temporary store, passing partly digested food to the intestine at intervals. A ring or *sphincter* muscle controls the outflow of food. Another sphincter at the inlet of the oesophagus prevents food passing up the oesophagus when the stomach contracts.

First loop of *small intestine* is the duodenum. This receives creamy fluid *(chyme)* from stomach. Digestive juice from *pancreas* and *bile* from *gall bladder* produced by the *liver* is released onto the food. Pancreatic juice contains three enzymes: *trypsin* (a mixture of enzymes) which acts on proteins breaking them down to peptones and these to *amino acids*, an *amylase* breaks down starch to maltose and a lipase fats to *fatty acids* and *glycerol*. Bile is a watery green fluid which causes large fat droplets to break up into smaller ones by reducing surface tension;

FOOD, FEEDING AND DIGESTION 21

Fig 8. Human digestive system

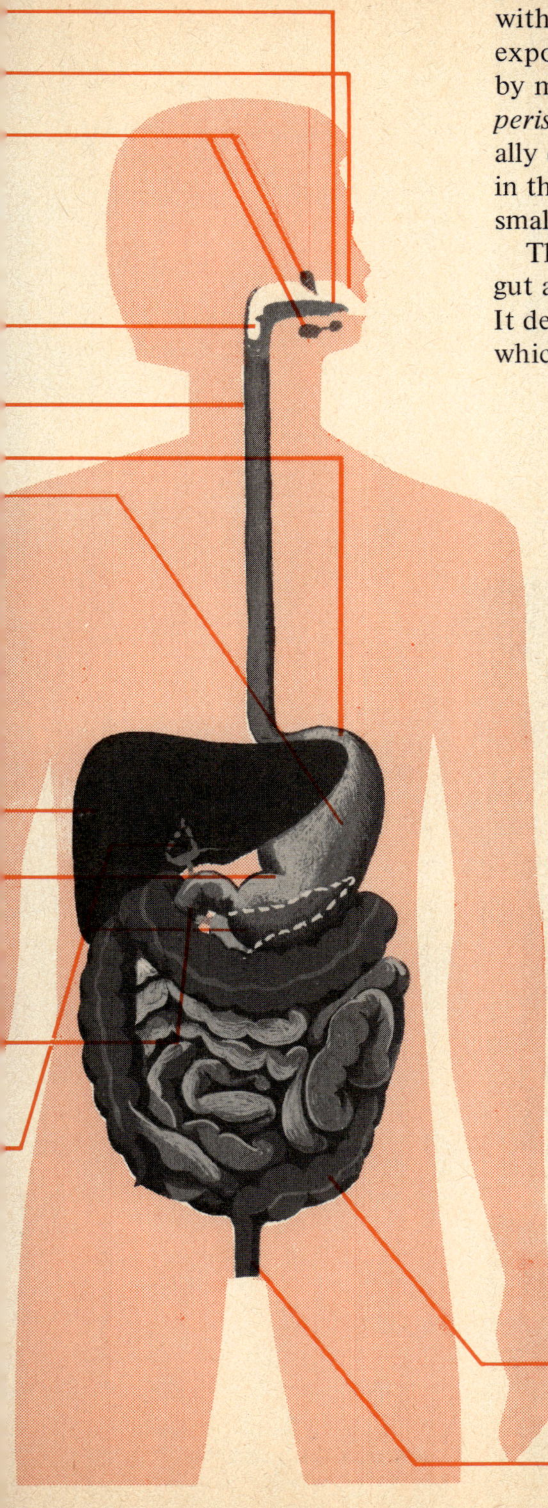

The breaking up of the food in the mouth into smaller particles ensures that as much of it is brought into contact with the saliva as possible. It is thoroughly wetted and exposed to the action of ptyalin. The food is moved along by muscular contraction of the gut wall. This is called *peristalsis*, and it also helps in the stomach to mix the partially digested food into a paste. Little of the food is absorbed in the stomach itself. Most of the digestion occurs in the small intestine where most of the absorption also takes place.

The diagram summarises the changes that occur in the gut as the food is moved along from one part to another. It details the main digestive enzymes, the food substances on which they act, and the glands which produce the enzymes.

also helps neutralise acid produced by stomach so that enzymes from pancreas and those produced by cells of small intestine wall can act more effectively.

Several enzymes produce complete digestion of food, prior to its being absorbed into bloodstream. *Erepsin* converts proteoses and peptones (fragments of protein molecules) to amino acids, *lipase* fats to fatty acids and glycerol, several carbohydrate-digesting enzymes convert the larger sugar molecules to simple sugars.

The stomach and small intestine glands produce a lot of mucus which protects the gut lining from the digestive enzymes, preventing it from being digested. Both pepsin and trypsin are produced in inactive forms which become active only when they come into contact with the chemicals in the cavity of the gut. The control of enzyme and fluid output by the gut lining cells is partly chemical through hormones and the direct presence of food substances, and partly through nerves. For instance, acid in the intestine causes the release of a hormone *secretin*, which acts on the pancreas causing it to release large amounts of watery digestive fluid.

In the *large intestine* water and some salts are absorbed into the bloodstream, leaving undigested food which is slowly converted into *faeces*.

The faeces are expelled through the *anus* from the *rectum*.

The digestion of egg white by pepsin

1 Add a little egg white to a boiling tube half full of distilled water and mix thoroughly. Boil the mixture and continue stirring. The egg white clots (coagulates) and the pieces are broken up into small particles by stirring.

2 After allowing the mixture to cool, equal portions are poured into six boiling tubes. Tube 1: add a few drops of dilute hydrochloric acid. Tube 2: add a little pepsin. Tube 3: add a little pepsin plus a few drops of dilute hydrochloric acid. Tube 4: Add a little pepsin plus a few drops of sodium bicarbonate solution (alkali). Tube 5: add a few drops of sodium bicarbonate solution. Tube 6: add a few drops of dilute hydrochloric acid plus a little pepsin that has previously been boiled.

3 The six tubes should be placed in a water bath at body temperature (approximately 36°C or 98°F) for half an hour and then examined.

4 What do you observe? How do you account for the differences between tubes 3 and 6?

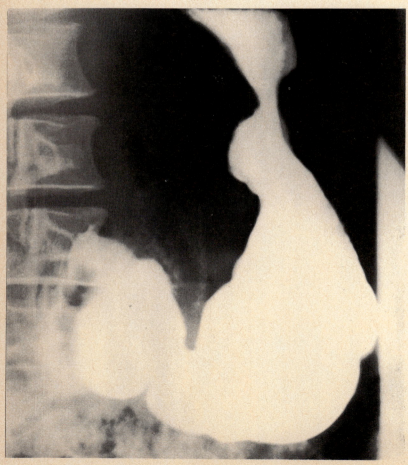

Fig 9. X-ray photograph of human stomach. X-rays taken at intervals show the stomach to change shape considerably as the peristaltic waves move across it

by courtesy of St. Bartholomew's Hospital and Medical College

FOOD, FEEDING AND DIGESTION

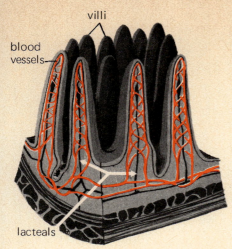

Fig 10. Villi in the wall of the small intestine—cut away to show their blood supply and the lacteals highly magnified

Absorption

The lining of the small intestine has numerous finger-like projections called *villi* (singular *villus*) which greatly increase its surface area and make for speedy and efficient absorption of the products of digestion. Each villus is richly supplied with blood capillaries and has a fat-collecting vessel or *lacteal*. The blood vessels receive amino acids (from proteins) and sugars (from starchy foods) via the outer cells of the villi, and most of the fatty acids (derived from fat) reform as fat and pass into the lacteals which are connected to a series of lymph spaces in the gut wall. This lymph passes through a system of lymph vessels to a main blood vessel entering the heart, from which it is distributed to all parts of the body. It may there be stored or used as fuel for providing energy. The blood capillaries join to form the *hepatic portal vein* which carries the amino acids and sugars to the liver.

The large intestine is largely responsible for the absorption of water still in the digested food.

The liver

This, the largest gland in the body, acts as a sorting office between the gut blood vessels and the body tissues. Both the quality and quantity of materials in the blood leaving the liver are regulated by it. It is strategically situated underneath the diaphragm and next to the stomach and intestine. Its main role is to manage foodstuffs. It stores carbohydrates and fat, converting them to the substances required by the tissues—sugar to supply energy, fat to supply energy or for storage.

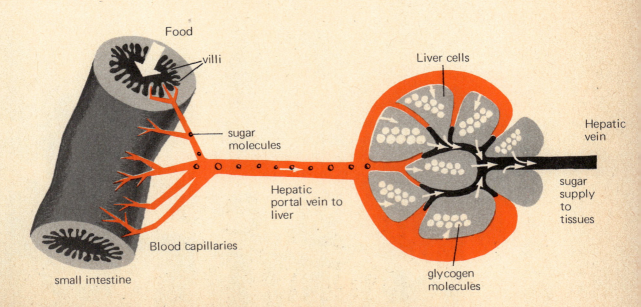

Fig 11. Diagram showing the main function of the liver as a sorting office between the gut blood vessels and the body tissues

Amino acids above the body's requirements cannot be stored; they are *deaminated* with the ultimate formation of carbohydrates, and the incorporation of nitrogen in urea, a waste product that is removed from the blood by the kidneys.

Sugars are stored in the liver in the form of *glycogen* or animal starch. Fatty acids are converted to fat or burnt to supply energy for chemical processes, and heat to help maintain the high body temperature. The products of fat oxidation can be reassembled as carbohydrates. The latter can be formed, therefore, from both fat and protein.

Another major activity of the liver is the production of *bile,* stored in the *gall bladder.* When food enters the small intestine from the stomach the bile is released.

The production of heat has been mentioned; this can be distributed to the tissues by the blood. Liver cells also produce vitamin A, they store iron and copper, and, most important, break down the harmful substances or toxins produced by bacteria, the dead bacteria themselves and other harmful substances such as alcohol.

Producing enough food

In just over a hundred years the earth's population has trebled to more than 3,000 million. It is expected to reach 6,000 million by 2000 AD. With a large proportion of today's population inadequately fed there is increasing alarm as to whether we shall be able to produce enough food for a greatly increased population. The earth's food supply can undoubtedly be increased, but the problem is more one of distributing the present wealth of food equally among the whole population. At the moment western countries and Australasia enjoy a high standard of living, whilst the people of some Asian and African countries are mostly undernourished.

At present only about a quarter of the cultivable land is cultivated, and much of that is not put to the best use. Relatively little is known of the sea's full potential, except that it is not being fully realised at the moment. The sea is a rich source of protein—fish is an important example

Fig 12. Population growth —will it be 6000 million by 2000 AD?

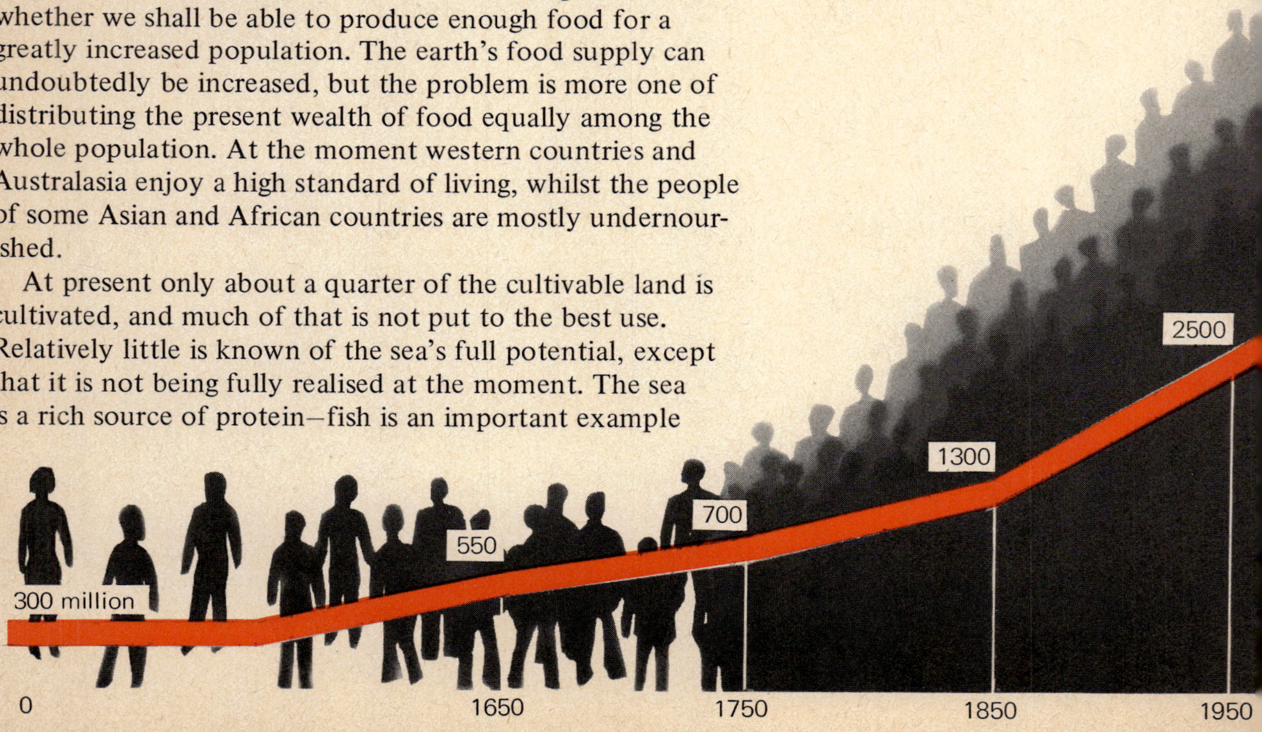

with 50,000,000 tons caught each year. In fact, many species of fish are overfished and have declined drastically in numbers. But, apart from the culture of mussels and oysters in a few sheltered coastal areas and catches of turtles, crabs, lobsters and the like, the other resources are largely untapped. Experiments are taking place to try to culture algae in sufficient quantities to provide protein. This is just one of the many ways in which scientists are trying to increase food production from new sources. Also important is to improve the present use of farmland and to bring other land into cultivation. The use of fertilizers has led to high increases in farm yields, but there is no replacement of humus—decayed organic remains— and the long term effects of their continued use on the numbers and balance of soil bacteria and other organisms needed to maintain 'healthy' soil is something that we will have to watch closely. The practice of ploughing in cereal stubble, and crops such as clover, does help to improve the soil content and its consistency, but more food could be grown in many parts of the world simply by introducing modern machinery. Laborious hand methods of cultivation are still common in the poorer countries. FAO, the Food and Agricultural Organisation of the United Nations Organisation, gives agricultural aid to a number of backward countries. It provides advisers, machinery, seeds and fertilizers, helping to introduce farm programmes that have long and short term benefits. Huge irrigation schemes have been undertaken in dry and desert regions in an attempt to recreate the fertile conditions that once existed in many of these areas. They have introduced newer and heavier yielding varieties of crops, ones that are more disease and drought resistant and so on.

But there is clearly a need for the same kind of 'farm' management of the sea as there is on land. This will have to be on an international basis for it to be successful. At the moment some countries fail to agree even on fishing limits. Whaling was once widespread in northern waters, but overfishing almost exhausted the stocks of some kinds of whale and whaling there was no longer worthwhile. The fleets wasted away. The same thing is happening in southern oceans—stocks of the giant blue whales, for example, are getting precariously low and the species is increasingly in danger of extinction. The future of the whaling fleets must be in doubt too. The countries concerned must come to their senses before all the whales and whaling fleets disappear. Because of the present overfishing for fish, international fishing agreements must be made and kept if the fishing fleets are not to go the way of many of the whaling fleets.

Preserving foods

Preventing food from going bad is a considerable problem nowadays with the mass transporting of food often from countries on one side of the world to another. Much of Britain's food is imported with large quantities of meat and butter shipped from Australia and New Zealand and beef from Brazil and Argentina—journeys taking several weeks. During this time the food is kept cool in specially refrigerated holds. At the dockside meat may be stored for a further three months before it is distributed to shops in specially refrigerated or insulated vehicles.

Keeping food cool is an important way of preserving it. But why does food go bad?

Place in several saucers on a windowsill; a piece of bread, a piece of bread moistened with a little water, an apple and a plum, a nob of butter and a small piece of cheese. Leave them for several days. Write down any changes that you observe in each of the foods.

Fig 13. A New Zealand Shipping Company's refrigerated cargo ship discharging its cargo of lamb

by courtesy of the New Zealand Lamb Information Bureau

Why foodstuffs spoil
Foodstuffs spoil because they:
1 dry due to loss of moisture
2 become contaminated or eaten by insects or other animals
3 may be affected by bacteria and fungi eating the chemicals of the foodstuffs to obtain energy
4 become rancid due to contact with the air
5 overripen due to chemical processes continuing, as with fruit

The aims of food preservation
Any method of preserving food aims to prevent or restrict to a minimum the processes or organisms that cause it to spoil. There are four basic methods of achieving this:
1 To remove water (as in drying)
2 The application of cold (as in quick freezing)
3 The application of heat (as in bottling and canning)
4 The addition of substances that restrict or prevent the growth of germs (eg salts, acids and certain preservatives—as in pickling)

Refrigeration
When food is kept cool below $-10°C$ chemical reactions in the food are stopped, ripening processes are halted and bacteria and other organisms, though not killed, are inactivated. Meat is stored and shipped from one country to another at $-10°C$ or below. It can be kept for up to three months in the dockside warehouse without losing flavour or drying. Fruit must be at cool rather than cold temperatures—apples $-0.6°C$ to $4.4°C$ for instance—just low enough to reduce the action of bacteria and fungi and to slow down the ripening processes. At too low temperatures the sap freezes, destroying its structure and consistency. When a food containing moisture is frozen the ice crystals formed in the food take up more space than the liquid water (water expands when it freezes). In meat, and fruit for instance, the ice crystals may rupture the cells of the tissues causing a loss of fluid when the food is thawed besides breaking down the actual structure of the food. This is particularly so when the food is frozen slowly, for large ice crystals form (see diagram overleaf).

Quick Frozen Food
In 1929, however, Clarence Birdseye, discovered that if food was frozen quickly (quick frozen) then many tiny ice crystals were formed without such noticeable expansion of the cell contents forcing the cell walls to rupture. The flavour of the food was retained. Today Birdseye's discovery has wide applications and we take frozen foods for granted.

Fig 14. Quick freezing fish

Fig 15.
A—Large ice crystals formed by slow freezing
B—Small ice crystals formed by quick freezing

Accelerated Freeze Drying

A recent advance on quick freezing is *accelerated freeze drying*. The food is dried then frozen even more quickly than by quick freezing. The foods are usually produced in powdered form—e.g. milk, coffee—and they can be reconstituted by adding water.

If some washing is hung out on a line in very cold weather, it will dry even though it may freeze. The water evaporates, although the ice does not melt, and the clothes are freeze dried.

Fig 17 Canning peas

Fig 16. On a cold day clothes will dry even when frozen: they are freeze dried

Food contains large amounts of water. When it is freeze dried it decreases considerably in volume and has a shrivelled appearance. Providing it remains dry it will not go bad: to keep moisture out when it is stored—it is not necessary to keep it in a refrigerator—it is put in waterproof packaging. Water is added only when using it. It then regains the appearance it had before it was dried

Nowadays powdered soups, whole meals, stews, chicken, mushrooms and many other kinds of food are preserved by accelerated freeze drying. The food is first quick frozen so that the cells retain their shape and is then placed in a vacuum chamber in which the water is removed. Food prepared in this way can be kept for three years before it is used.

Canning

Food is also preserved by *canning*. Vegetables, fruit and many other foods are canned, that is, sealed in cans from which air has been excluded and in which germs cannot grow and multiply. This method of preserving food was discovered by a Frenchman, Nicholas Appert, in 1809. He used bottles sealed with corks. An Englishman, Peter Durand, patented the first tin can in 1810. The illustration shows the various processes of canning.

Pasteurisation

Milk for bottling is subjected to a special process known as *pasteurisation*. In this it is heated in special equipment (see illustrations) up to a temperature of 160°F—enough to kill even the most resistant pathogens without destroying the food value or affecting the flavour.

Hygiene

Wrapping food helps to keep it clean and also to stop it from being contaminated by bacteria and other organisms. But too much food is still unrefrigerated, handled by hand and left exposed to flies and other insects. Because certain organisms in bad food and in cooked and uncooked food can cause serious, even fatal illnesses, cleanliness is most important. All who work in food shops or who handle or prepare food in factories, hotels and elsewhere must ensure that their hands are regularly washed, particularly after using the toilet.

Fig 18. Pasteurisation plant

by courtesy of Express Dairies

Fig 19. Biscuit packs overwrapped with polypropylene film

by courtesy of ICI Ltd

Fig 20. Food production line—operators in white coats and with hair covered

by courtesy of Smedleys

3 Breathing and respiration

The movements of breathing are one of the most obvious signs of life. But why do we breathe and how do we breathe? What happens to the air that we breathe in? How often do we breathe? What affects our rate of breathing? We know some of the answers for certain but for others we can only give the most likely explanations based on our present knowledge. It is important in science to appreciate the difference between something that has been established as fact and something which is opinion based on available evidence.

The breathing system

A rat is a mammal and therefore its basic anatomy will be very similar to ours. Examine the mouth, neck and chest of a freshly killed rat before and after the ribs and their muscles have been carefully cut away to expose the contents of the chest. Insert a blowpipe into the windpipe of the rat through its mouth and blow down it. What happens? When you stop blowing what happens? What prevents the windpipe from collapsing? Compare the structure of the windpipe with that of a piece of flexible car hose or a similar pipe.

The lungs are pinkish-red in colour, not bright red—why do you think this is so? Cut a slice of lung tissue off one of the rat's lungs. Squeeze this lung gently and observe what happens at the lung's cut surface. Squeeze the slice of lung tissue under water. What do you see?

If you feel your own ribs and windpipe and look into your throat in a mirror you can find out something about your own breathing system. The movements of your ribs as you breathe in and out will also give you some clues as to what happens during breathing.

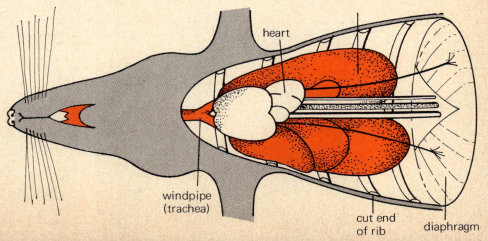

Fig 21. Dissection of the chest of a rat

The mechanics of breathing

Place the palm faces of your fingers on your ribs firmly, breathe in deeply and then breathe out again. What did you feel happen to your ribs? Keeping your fingers on your ribs breathe in deeply, forcing out your stomach muscles. What happened to your ribs? When you breathe using your stomach muscles do you feel any difference to your rib movements when first holding your uppermost ribs and then lower ribs? Asthma sufferers have to learn to breathe by pushing out their stomach muscles in this way. You will understand why from what follows.

Compare the structure of the rat's thorax with that of the model illustrated right. When the rubber sheet is pulled downwards what happens to the balloons? When the sheet is released, what happens? Why do you think the balloons fill and then collapse again? What action that you have previously observed when holding your ribs is not indicated by the model? When you held your ribs and breathed by pushing out your stomach muscles there was little movement of your ribs compared with the more usual way of breathing. What structure was principally involved in air entering your lungs? Compare this with the action of the model.

When you held your ribs as you breathed in normally they moved upwards and outwards. The ribs, like all movable bones, are moved by the action of muscles. The diagram shows how the rib muscles are arranged, where the ribs pivot on the backbone and how they are joined to the breastbone or sternum in front. How do you think the muscles act during breathing movements? Try to devise a model using wooden strips with elastic bands to represent the muscles.

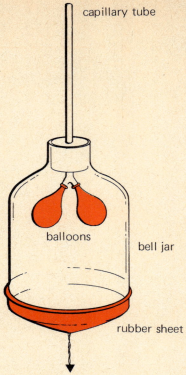

Fig 22.
Model showing breathing mechanism

Air exchange in breathing

Make up the two pieces of apparatus shown in the diagram and, with normal breaths, breathe in and out through them as indicated. How many breaths out were needed to turn the lime water milky? How many breaths in were required to turn the lime water in the other tube equally milky? Carbon dioxide turns lime water milky. How much carbon dioxide is present in expired air (air breathed out) compared with inspired air (air breathed in)? What do the differences tell you about the workings of the body? Note that the same amounts and same concentration of lime water should be used in each tube. Why do you think this is? Should the same person breathe into and out of the tubes? Why?

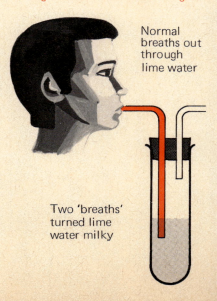

Fig 23. Lime water breathing test

BREATHING AND RESPIRATION

The composition of inspired and expired air

Substance or factor	Inspired air	Expired air
Oxygen	20-21%	16-17%
Carbon dioxide	0.03%	4% approx.
Nitrogen	79% approx.	79% approx.
Water vapour	Variable quantity	Nearly saturated
Temperature	Variable	Near to body temperature

From the table showing the composition of inspired and expired air it is clear that two things happen during breathing: the uptake of oxygen from the air and the output of carbon dioxide.

The human breathing system—its structure

Basically the breathing system is an airtight box containing the paired lungs which are in communication with the atmosphere by way of the windpipe and the mouth and nostrils. The airtight box can be expanded by the action of the rib muscles and the diaphragm. The pressure inside the box is then reduced and, atmospheric pressure now being greater than the pressure pushing on the lungs, air enters the lungs and inflates them. On breathing out, relaxation of the rib muscles and diaphragm, and the return of the stretched elastic fibres of the lung tissue to their original length, causes used air in the lungs to be forced out. The flexibility of the lung tissue is the most important factor in getting rid of the used air. During an attack of asthma tiny muscle fibres in the lung walls contract, or go into spasm, seriously reducing the lung's elasticity so that breathing out is difficult.

Structurally each lung and the main tube to it might be compared with a small tree covered in a polythene bag. The trunk represents the *bronchus* (plural bronchi), the branches the *bronchioles*, and the leaves the air sacs or *alveoli*. The polythene bag represents the outer covering or *pleura*. This becomes inflamed in the condition of pleurisy and the inner linings of the lungs in pneumonia.

The walls of the alveoli are covered in tiny blood capillaries and, since the walls are very thin, oxygen dissolving in the layer of mucus coating their inner surfaces can pass through into the blood very readily. Carbon dioxide can pass in the reverse direction. Why should oxygen pass in and carbon dioxide out in this way?

If you place some potassium permanganate crystals carefully at the bottom of a beaker of water and leave it, eventually the whole of the water will become coloured. (Care must be taken to make sure that no convection currents can cause

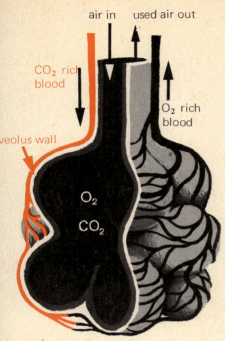

Fig 24. Diagram showing structure of alveoli and movement of air, oxygen and CO_2

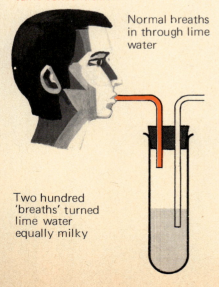

equal volume of lime water same concentration

Normal breaths in through lime water

Two hundred 'breaths' turned lime water equally milky

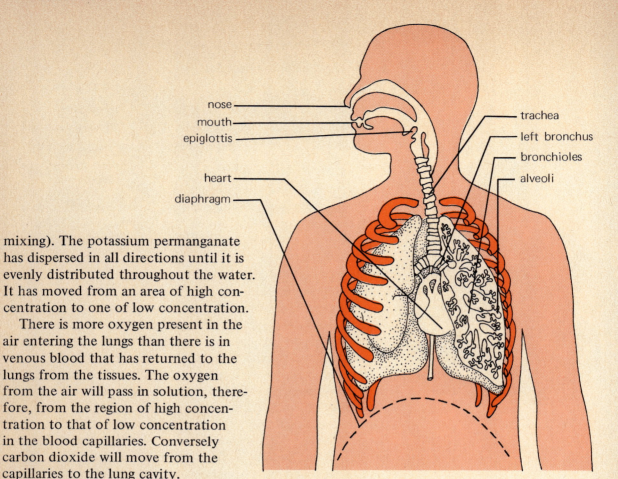

mixing). The potassium permanganate has dispersed in all directions until it is evenly distributed throughout the water. It has moved from an area of high concentration to one of low concentration.

There is more oxygen present in the air entering the lungs than there is in venous blood that has returned to the lungs from the tissues. The oxygen from the air will pass in solution, therefore, from the region of high concentration to that of low concentration in the blood capillaries. Conversely carbon dioxide will move from the capillaries to the lung cavity.

The opposite exchange takes place at the tissues. Blood rich in oxygen is pumped round the body to the tissues which will have less oxygen since they are continually using up their supply. So oxygen will pass from the blood to the tissues. The carbon dioxide waste produced by the tissues will pass from them into the bloodstream.

It should be stressed that there is an enormous number of air sacs in each human lung and the total area of their

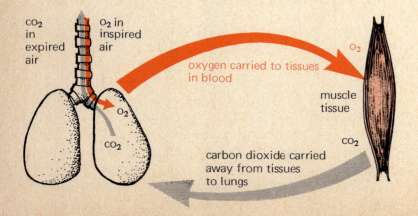

Fig 26. Diagram showing exchange of gases in lungs and tissues

inner surfaces is very great. This is necessary because the lungs are *blind* sacs; air containing oxygen must enter the lungs through the same passages that carbon dioxide laden air must leave. This arrangement is not as efficient as a *through system* would be. In a through system oxygen-rich air is continually passing over the respiratory surfaces. The network of capillaries enmeshing each air sac presents a large surface through which oxygen can pass.

Recording breathing movements

Using the apparatus shown (see Fig 27) it is possible to obtain a trace of the breathing movements. These can be taken while you are sitting down (i.e. at rest) and the number of breaths taken in a given time recorded by marking time intervals on the trace. If you were to step on and off a chair, say, twenty times in quick succession, and then your breathing movements were recorded what sort of trace would you expect? If after excercise of this kind you were to breathe in and out through the apparatus shown on page 32 you can compare how many breaths produce equal milkiness of the lime water compared with normal breaths. What will this tell you about your body processes?

Clearly the more work that your body does the greater will be the demand for oxygen. You breathe more deeply and more quickly. The traces on the smoked drum will show this. If you feel your ribs after exercise you will quite readily detect the greater movement associated with deeper breathing. But it is no use the chest working to take in more oxygen if the body is unable to get the oxygen into the blood. For this reason the heartbeat will increase in order to increase the volume of blood passing through the lungs and reaching the tissues in a given time.

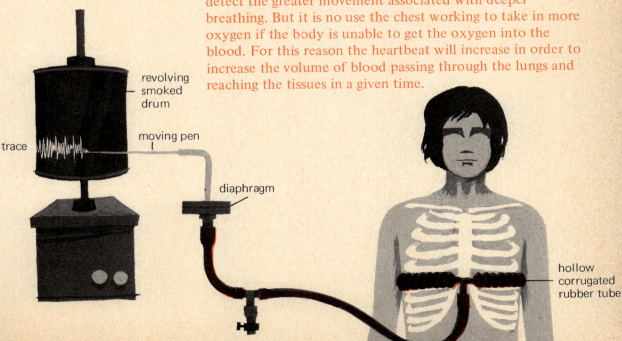

Fig 27. Recording breathing movements

In working at a faster rate the tissues produce more waste carbon dioxide. The greater volume of blood moving round the body results in more efficient removal of this carbon dioxide through the lungs.

Respiration

When work is done the body consumes oxygen and produces carbon dioxide. Oxygen is obtained at inspiration and carbon dioxide removed at expiration. We know that there are other natural processes requiring oxygen and producing carbon dioxide. If sugar, for instance, is burnt in air oxygen is used up, carbon dioxide is produced and heat released. Physiologists have carried out experiments to investigate how the body uses oxygen, and how it obtains energy. Doing work requires energy. Our muscles do work in moving our legs when we walk; they use energy.

Muscle action can be investigated in a number of ways. Changes in the amounts of substances in the muscles as a result of work can be determined chemically. Other methods may involve measuring the heat output of a muscle or tracing the chemical pathway of the radioactive version (isotope) of a chemical thought to be concerned with muscle action. If the quantities of chemicals in the blood going into and leaving a muscle are analysed, any differences will give some indication of chemical changes within the muscle. Blood leaving a working muscle contains less oxygen, less sugar and more carbon dioxide than blood entering the muscle. If the blood supply to a working muscle is stopped the muscle fatigues more quickly than when the blood supply is maintained. What do these observations tell you about the working of muscles?

It is possible to remove a muscle from a freshly killed animal such as a frog. By giving the muscle an electric shock it can be made to contract and lift a small weight. If the muscle is stimulated repeatedly it will continue to contract for a time but the force of the contractions gets less and eventually it fails to contract. If it is left for a while to recover in air or pure oxygen it will contract again upon stimulation. It will not recover in an atmosphere of nitrogen. The muscle does not fatigue so quickly if it is stimulated in an atmosphere of pure oxygen rather than air, but fatigues more quickly if it is stimulated in an atmosphere of pure nitrogen. The amount of sugar in the muscle decreases as a result of contraction and heat is produced. What do these facts tell you about muscle chemistry?

The chemical changes that happen in muscles and other tissues, in which a substance (sugar) containing carbon, hydrogen and oxygen is broken down in the presence of oxygen, are called respiration. Wherever respiration takes place energy is released, and water and carbon dioxide are formed. The burning of sugar has been mentioned and the overall chemical reaction is similar to respiration. But there are differences. Heat is not always produced in respiration and respiration will continue for a time in the absence of oxygen. Sugar burns at a very much higher temperature than that at which the tissues work. The chemical reaction described here for respiration is a great simplification. Respiration is not a single process but involves a variety of complicated chemical processes in which a number of chemical substances take part, particularly substances containing phosphate; each process is controlled by an enzyme.

The blood and breathing

The role of the blood in carrying oxygen from the lungs to the tissues has been described, but how is oxygen carried in the blood?

It is possible to measure the quantity of oxygen in blood by chemical means. Like sea water, blood contains a mixture of salts. Yet sea water exposed to air contains one per cent of oxygen while blood exposed to the air will contain 19 per cent of oxygen. This compares with about 20 per cent oxygen in air itself. Sea water and blood are both liquids but blood contains cells—red and white blood cells—and the red cells contain a *pigment*. Which of these facts might account for the greater quantity of oxygen that the blood can carry compared with sea water? Look at the additional information that follows.

After the red cells have been removed from the blood the oxygen content is just under one per cent—about the same as in sea water. The oxygen content of the red cells can be measured chemically and it is also possible to release the red pigment (*haemoglobin*) from the cells and measure the quantity of oxygen it carries. About 18% is obtained in each case. Notice also that blood arriving at the lungs which is poor in oxygen is a dull red colour, whilst the reoxygenated blood leaving the lungs is a bright red colour. What does the information tell you about the way that oxygen is carried in the blood?

In humans the dull red pigment, *haemoglobin*, is present in the red cells. Oxygen in the blood combines with haemoglobin to form *oxyhaemoglobin,* which is a bright red colour. At the tissues the blood releases its oxygen: oxyhaemoglobin reverts to haemoglobin and the blood becomes a dull red colour again. Most of the oxygen is carried in the red cells, a little in solution in the plasma. The blood temperature in man is about 36°C; warm-blooded creatures have very active tissues and require large quantities of oxygen. The tissue cells could not function efficiently if we lacked an oxygen-carrying pigment in the blood since they would receive insufficient oxygen from that carried in the plasma alone.

The Rhesus Factor

The rhesus factor is a group of substances present in the red blood cells of most people (85% or more). It is so named because it was first discovered in the rhesus monkey. People whose red cells contain the rhesus factor are said to be rhesus positive (Rh+); those lacking it are rhesus negative (Rh−). If rhesus positive blood is transfused into someone with rhesus negative blood the foreign Rh+ blood is treated, just as invading germs would be, by the production of protective chemicals (*antibodies*) that destroy the rhesus factor. This may not be too serious with a first small transfusion but, because the antibodies produced remain in the blood, the Rh+ blood of a further transfusion might be more vigorously attacked with more serious consequences. The situation may be especially critical for an unborn child with Rh+ blood whose mother is Rh−, for some of the baby's blood may get into the mother's blood stream triggering off the production of antibodies. They may not harm the first child (unless the mother has previously received a transfusion of Rh+ blood) but, because the antibodies are already in the blood, the second child may suffer as its red blood cells will be subjected to attack by the antibodies. This results in a condition called *haemolytic anaemia* and the condition, once always fatal, has to be relieved by the newborn child receiving a complete transfusion of Rh− blood; all its blood is replaced.

The child's body will eventually produce its own Rh+ blood and the Rh− supply it received will be gradually destroyed before it can produce antibodies.

Because of the dangers of an unborn child being affected an expectant mother should always be tested to see if she has Rh− blood. Genes from both parents control the rhesus factor and it is common in a Rh− mother to have a Rh+ child, therefore.

4 The heart and circulation

We are all aware of the very vigorous and rapid beating of the heart after violent exercise, yet while resting in a chair we barely notice its activity. The heart is an organ whose action changes to cope with the varying demands made on it by other parts of the body. During exercise our muscles have to work much harder; their oxygen and fuel requirements are higher and more blood has to be pumped to the muscles to supply these substances. Similarly more waste substances are produced and the increased blood flow through the muscle helps in their removal. Although the muscle blood supply increases during exercise, that to other parts of the body (e.g. the gut) is decreased. For this reason you should never take vigorous exercise too soon after a heavy meal.

It is possible to learn a great deal about the blood system by simple experiments and observations. Early in the seventeenth century William Harvey, an English physician, introduced the experimental approach to medicine and biology. Prior to his work it was thought that the blood merely flowed and ebbed to and from the heart—circulation had not been discovered. Although he had no microscope with which to show the existence of capillaries connecting the arteries and veins, by painstaking dissection, careful observation and experiments, Harvey was able to show the heart to be a hollow, muscular organ which pumps the blood into the arteries in pulses. He showed too that the veins had valves to prevent blood flowing back towards the extremities of the body. When he measured the heart's output at each beat he was able to show that the whole of the blood in the body is pumped through the heart in a very short time. Over a longer period the same blood must pass through the heart again and again. The only way it could flow back to the heart is along the veins. Clearly the blood must circulate.

It was not until after Harvey's death in 1657 that the Italian microscopist, Marcello Malpighi, one of the first investigators using a microscope, discovered the capillaries; too fine to be seen by the naked eye.

40 HUMAN BIOLOGY

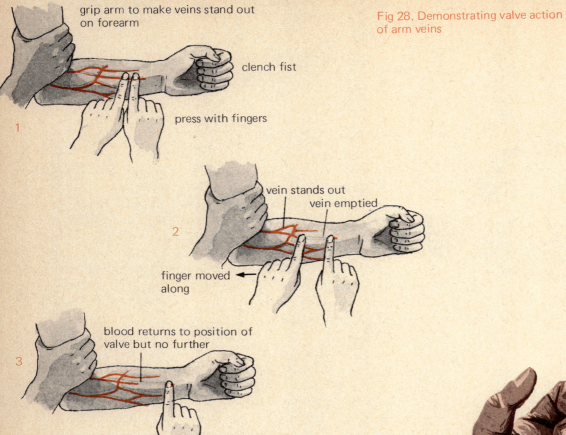

Fig 28. Demonstrating valve action of arm veins

Measurement of pulse rate

When the heart contracts, blood is forced out through the *aorta* under pressure, and as the blood moves from the aorta to the other arteries that branch off it to the limbs and other parts of the body a pressure wave travels along the arteries. The movement of the pressure wave can be felt quite easily as the *pulse* wherever an artery is close to the skin as at the wrist (see illustration). Counting the number of pulses in a minute (or half a minute and multiplying by two) gives the rate of heartbeat. Each member of the class should record the pulse of his neighbour when he is seated. Count the pulse again after quickly stepping on and off a stool twenty times, say. Make a histogram from the information obtained and from it work out the average heartbeat of the class, and the fastest and slowest heartbeats. Do you think there is any

Fig 29. Taking the pulse

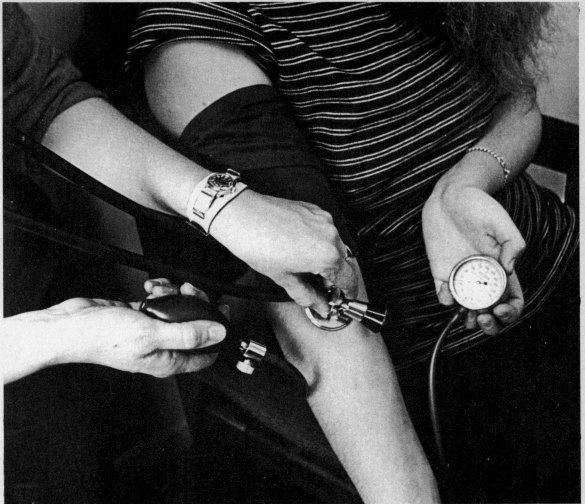

Fig 30. Measuring blood pressure

Angela Phillips

relationship between a person's athletic ability, especially as a cross country runner, and his or her heartbeat? Does the average boy's heartbeat differ from that of the girls? What should you ensure when recording the heartbeat following stepping on and off the stool if the results for each person are to be comparable?

If after stepping on and off the stool or after any other energetic exercise the pulse rate is taken at equal intervals from ½ minute to 1 minute after the end of the exercise, 1 to 1½, 1½ to 2, 2½ to 3, 3½ to 4, 4½ to 5 minutes a graph can be plotted showing pulse rate against time after exercise. Is there any relationship between the type of curve (i.e. the speed of recovery) and a person's cross country performance or his or her physical build? Why doesn't the pulse rate return to normal immediately the exercise stops?

The structure of the heart

The human heart is a hollow, muscular sac, about the size of an average man's fist (slightly smaller in women), with four compartments. It is situated underneath the breastbone and between the lungs. Its four compartments are arranged two in each of the two halves of the heart. The right side of the heart comprises the *right auricle* and *right ventricle*, and the left the *left auricle* and *left ventricle*. The right auricle, the upper right chamber, receives from the tissues blood poor in oxygen—it is a collecting chamber. The blood passes from there into the right ventricle where it is pumped to the lungs for reoxygenation. It returns to the left side of the heart entering the upper chamber there, the left auricle. It passes into the left ventricle which contracts to pump it out of the heart through the aorta. Within the heart, therefore, blood low in oxygen and high in carbon dioxide content is kept separate from blood rich in oxygen and low in carbon dioxide returning from the lungs.

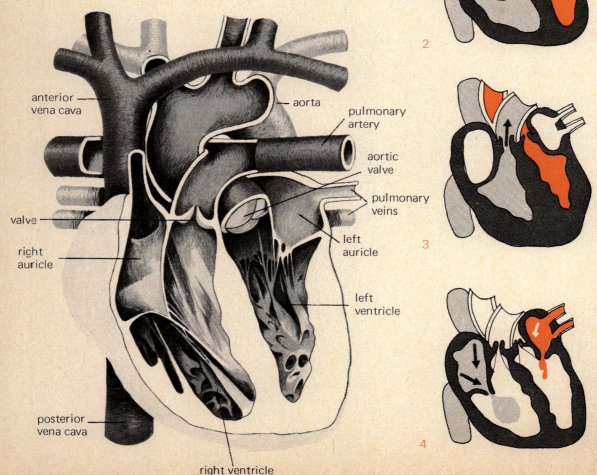

Fig 31. Cut-away section of heart

Human heart cycle

THE HEART AND CIRCULATION 43

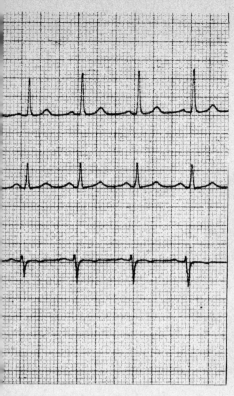

Fig 33. Electrocardiogram and ECG trace

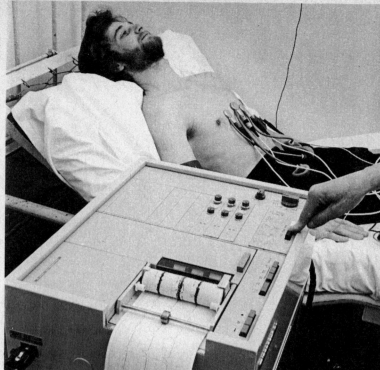

Fig 32. Diagram of heart cycle

1. Heart relaxes (between beats) both auricles fill with blood.
2. Auricles contract, valves open allowing blood to fill ventricles.
3. Ventricles contract forcing blood out of heart through the valves in the aorta and pulmonary artery
4. The heart relaxes again. Auricles fill and cycle is ready to start again.

Sometimes a baby is born whose oxygen-rich blood and oxygen-poor blood are not kept completely separate because of a heart defect. The baby's appearance is somewhat blue, because the blood is low in oxygen and the condition has the name of 'blue baby'.

Both auricles contract together just before the ventricles which then contract together. On average the heart contracts seventy times a minute in the resting adult. Each heartbeat takes about four-tenths of a second and is followed by a resting period of about the same length before the next contraction occurs. This ensures that a new contraction does not take place before the last one has finished. In some types of heart disease the beat loses its regularity; this can be checked by means of a small recording device, the electrocardiogram (ECG for short). When the heart is badly diseased it may be able to supply insufficient oxygen for the muscles to be very active. A person is unlikely to be able to play games and may be completely chairbound. Depending on the kind of heart damage and its extent, surgery may be able to correct the damaged condition, but the only recourse for the surgeon may be the complete replacement of the damaged heart with the heart of a person that has recently died (a heart transplant). The replacement heart must be undamaged of course.

Valves between the heart chambers and in the aorta prevent the blood from flowing backwards. When the auricles contract blood is forced through the valves into the ventricles, but when these contract the valves close so that blood can only pass to the lungs or the aorta. The valves may be diseased or fail to work properly. Heart surgeons have devised ways of inserting plastic valves with which they are able to replace the damaged valves. Heart valves from pigs have also been used successfully.

If you look at the heart diagram you will see that the muscular wall of the left ventricle is very much thicker than that of the right ventricle. Why do you think this is so?

The blood vessels

Arteries carry blood away from the heart; *veins* carry blood towards the heart. All arteries, except the pulmonary arteries, carry oxygenated blood. All veins, except the pulmonary veins, carry deoxygenated blood. The arteries branch many times to form smaller vessels called *arterioles* and these eventually branch to form in the tissues minute *capillaries* whose walls are only one cell thick. The capillaries eventually join up to form larger vessels, *venules*, and these join to form the veins carrying blood back to the heart.

The thin walls of the capillaries, which form a dense network in the tissues, allow blood rich in oxygen, food substances and other materials such as hormones to come into close contact with the tissue cells. The arterial blood pressure—derived from the heartbeat— forces sugar and other food materials from the blood into the tissue cells; oxygen passes out by diffusion. The pressure gradually drops as the blood passes through the capillary network until in the veins it is only one-tenth of its arterial value. Waste materials and water return because the osmotic pressure of the blood, that due to the blood proteins, is higher than the blood pressure due to the heartbeat. So the tissues are nourished and relieved of their waste products.

The venous blood pressure is not high enough to force blood from, say, the toes back to the heart. How does the venous blood return? Although the veins have thin and not very muscular walls they are able to contract to help drive the blood back to the heart. The heart has a slight sucking action, too. When muscles contract and relax, especially those in the limbs, they help to squeeze the veins and so propel blood to the heart and, since the veins have valves, the blood cannot flow backwards. When a patient is given a blood transfusion, or any other form of 'drip' is passed into a

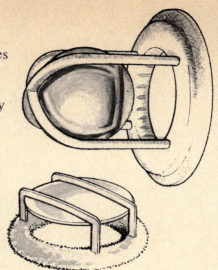

Fig 34. Two types of artificial replacement valves for the heart

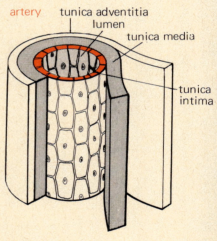

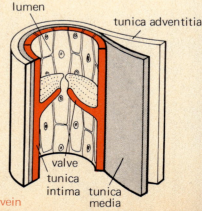

Fig 35. Sections of blood vessels

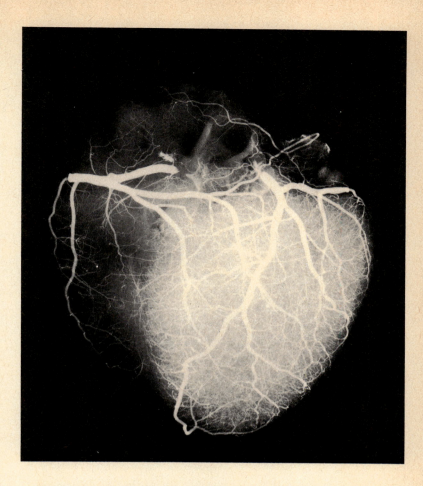

Fig 36. X-ray photograph of coronary arteries

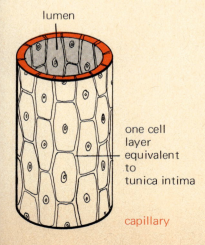

vein, the needle in the blood vessel should always point towards the heart. Why do you think this is so and why is a vein used and not an artery?

Heart muscle, unlike an arm muscle for example, is able to contract independently of the nervous system, but it does have a nerve supply. Many factors can affect the rate at which the heart beats: excitement and other forms of emotion, increased breathing rate, higher than usual amounts of carbon dioxide in the blood, lower amounts of oxygen, the quantity of blood returning to the right auricle and, of course, drugs. Nicotine inhaled from cigarette smoke increases the heart beat considerably, and this is one reason why doctors consider that smoking cigarettes is harmful. Like other tissues, heart muscle requires food, so it has its own blood system. The coronary arteries show up clearly on an X-ray picture when a dye has been injected into them. If a blood clot blocks one of the branches of the coronary artery the tissue beyond the clot is starved of oxygen and fuel and a heart attack may result. Look at the photograph.

The body fluids

Blood

The average adult male has about ninety pints of fluid in his body altogether; women and children have less. Of this about one tenth is blood. This red fluid is contained in the blood vessels and consists of a liquid *plasma* in which float the *white* and *red cells* or *corpuscles*. If a sample of blood is placed in a tube and the mixture centrifuged the cells, being heavier than the plasma, are thrown to the bottom of the tube. They can be seen to make up just under half the blood's volume. Most of the plasma consists of water. It is rich in substances derived from food—particularly salts and protein, and also contains glucose, fat, amino acids, urea (nitrogen-containing waste formed by the breakdown of excess protein), hormones, enzymes and antibodies– (substances produced by some of the white cells to help combat invading organisms).

Because plasma contains mostly water its properties closely resemble water. It plays an important part in the distribution to the rest of the body of heat produced by the muscles and the liver helping to maintain the high, constant body temperature because water gains and loses heat slowly.

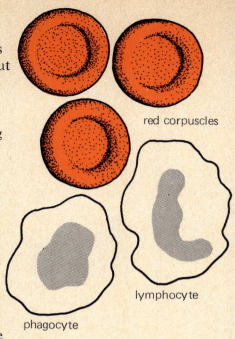

Fig 37. Blood cells (highly magnified)

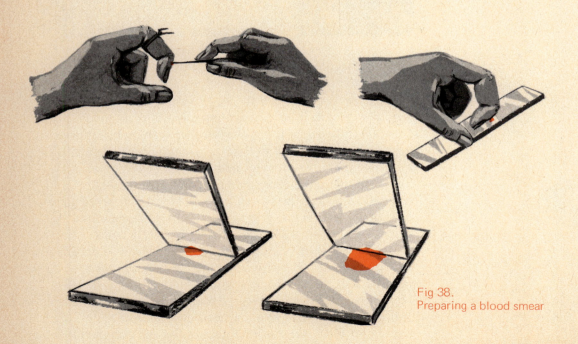

Fig 38. Preparing a blood smear

THE HEART AND CIRCULATION 47

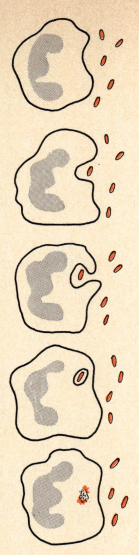

Fig 39. A phagocyte engulfing and digesting a bacterium

Fig 40. A lymphocyte producing antibodies to destroy bacteria

All the body tissues are consequently working under fairly constant conditions. Water is the universal solvent; more substances dissolve in it than in any other substance so that numerous chemical substances can be carried from one part of the body to another dissolved in the blood.

The red cells owe their colour to the red pigment, *haemoglobin*. They contain nearly all of the body's supply of this substance. Haemoglobin is a protein-containing substance which combines with oxygen. The oxygen which is absorbed by the blood in the lungs and transported by the blood to the tissues is carried by the haemoglobin. Apart from carrying oxygen the red cells carry a little carbon dioxide. Red cells have no nuclei and because of this their life is limited to about four months. After this time they disintegrate and are consumed by the blood's 'dustmen'—certain of the white cells called *phagocytes*. New cells are produced continuously in the bone marrow and stored in the spleen until required. An adult male has about 5 000 000 red cells in each cubic millimetre of blood (4 500 000 in women).

Apart from phagocytes there are several kinds of white cell which, in addition to breaking down old red cells, are responsible for attacking disease-causing bacteria, and for getting rid of dead bacteria and other dead cells.

Lymphocytes produce *antibodies*. These substances attack all kinds of foreign cells and play a vital part in protecting the body against invading organisms. This important action is a major difficulty in transplant operations, for when an organ such as a kidney is taken from one person and transplanted in another the lymphocytes produce antibodies which attack the cells of the transplanted organ because they recognize them as foreign. Drugs and radiation treatment help to suppress this natural reaction and allow the transplanted organ to 'take', but at the same time the body's natural defence against bacteria is removed. For this reason patients receiving transplants are kept in sterile conditions.

Much smaller than the red or white cells are the *platelets*. These tiny cell-like structures have an important role in blood clotting. When a blood vessel breaks they act like sandbags will to plug a breached dyke wall.

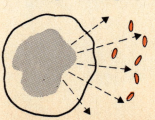

antibodies produced

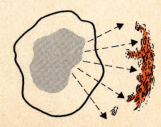

bacteria destroyed

The lymphatic system

Only about a tenth of the body's fluid total is blood. The spaces between the tissue cells contain fluid, as do the cells themselves. Fluid bathing the cells is in close communication with the blood capillaries and contains all the substances from the blood that the cells require to function efficiently. Waste substances pass from the cells into the fluid in the spaces and into the blood capillaries or alternatively into a special system of tubes, the *lymphatic system*.

This much-branched system ends in blind lymph capillaries slightly larger in diameter than blood capillaries. The lymphatics contain a fluid called *lymph* which is returned to the blood system by a major lymph vessel entering one of the main veins near the heart. Lymph is chemically similar to blood plasma though it contains very little protein. Lymph vessels are particularly well developed near the gut. Their finest branches in this region—*lacteals*—end in the villi of the small intestine and are important in the uptake of digested fat from the intestine (see page 23). Lymph vessels contain valves, similar to those of the veins, and they prevent the flow of lymph back away from the heart. The vessels do not contract, however. The lymph is moved slowly along mainly by the squeezing action of the body muscles when these contract.

The lymph system is essentially an extraordinarily efficient filter. Invading bacteria can squeeze between the cells of the lymph vessel walls and, when they reach swellings—*lymph nodes*—occurring at intervals along the lymph vessels, the phagocytes and lymphocytes there get to work. The lymph nodes may become swollen and painful when an infection occurs. For example, the 'glands' in the neck do so as a result of a sore throat. People who live in towns inhale large quantities of dust and other foreign particles. The lymph nodes in the lungs may eventually become black because of this.

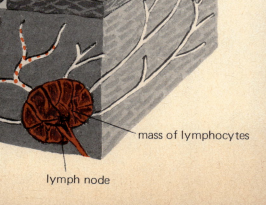

Fig 41. Section of skin showing the lymph system

bacteria entering through cut in skin

mass of lymphocytes

lymph vessels

lymph node

5 Excretion: the removal of waste

The body takes in a wide variety of chemicals; mostly food substances into the digestive system, but also air into the lungs. None of the required chemicals in these substances can be utilized by the body until they have passed into solution in which form they can enter the bloodstream. Food substances pass into solution as a result of digestion and oxygen enters the mucus layer lining the air sacs of the lungs and then passes into the bloodstream to be carried to the tissues. In the tissues some of the food materials are burnt with the oxygen to produce energy for the everyday processes of nerve and muscle action, repair and growth. Some molecules are stored for future use; some used as structural repair and growth materials. All processes requiring energy result in waste substances being produced. These waste products must be removed by the body, or the body's living processes could become poisoned. The removal of waste is called *excretion* and the major organs concerned are the *kidneys*. The kidneys are paired, bean-shaped structures situated in the abdomen just under the rib cage.

The work of the kidneys
Each kidney receives blood through the renal artery. The blood returns to the circulation through the renal vein. From each kidney a *ureter* carries urine to the bladder to be stored temporarily.

If an analysis is made of substances passing into each kidney via the renal artery and out through the renal vein and the ureter these are some of the facts that emerge. What do you think they show?
1 Blood in the renal artery contains about 3 parts of urea per ten thousand parts of blood
2 Urine in the ureter contains 2 parts urea per hundred parts urine
3 Blood in both artery and vein is rich in glucose
4 Urine in a healthy kidney normally contains no glucose
5 Blood contains blood cells and protein molecules
6 Urine contains no blood cells or protein, provided the kidney is healthy and undamaged

Remember that some substances dissolve in water (eg sugar) and others (eg protein) do not. If you were to pour a liquid containing say, chalk (insoluble) and glucose sugar (soluble) through a filter funnel containing filter paper, the insoluble substance would not pass through the filter paper but the soluble substance would.

The Structure of the Kidneys

If you cut a kidney in half lengthwise, two main zones can be distinguished: an outer *cortex* and an inner *medulla*. Encasing the whole kidney is a fatty envelope or *capsule*. Most of the kidney tissue consists of masses of tiny *tubules*. These link up to form larger *collecting tubes* which eventually join to form the *ureter*. The drawing of a tubule shows that it has a rich blood supply. Each tubule ends in a champagne-glass shaped structure whose walls are hollow. Within the cup—called the *Bowman's capsule*—of the tubule is a knot of capillaries,

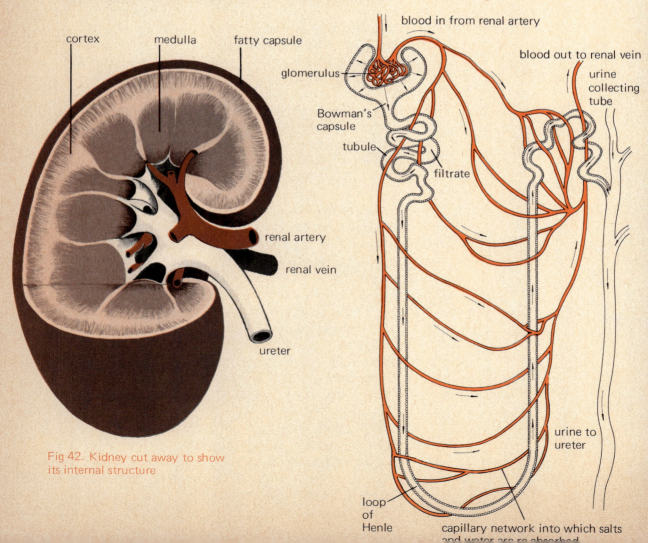

Fig 43. Diagram showing arrangement of single tubule

Fig 42. Kidney cut away to show its internal structure

small branches of the renal artery, called the *glomerulus*. Each Bowman's capsule and glomerulus is termed a *Malpighian body* of which there are more than a million in each kidney. The tube from each Bowman's capsule loops down into the medulla and becomes narrower—the *loop of Henle*. The tube then widens again to join other tubules which form collecting ducts. Eventually these join together forming the ureter.

This internal structure has been worked out by dissection, by taking successive thin tissue slices and injecting dyes and rubber solutions into the tubules to make casts, so building up a three-dimensional picture.

By inserting minute pipettes into the various parts of the capsule and tubule it is possible to extract fluid samples which can be analysed chemically. The table shows some of the major chemicals dissolved in blood plasma, in the fluid in the capsule, and in the urine.

	Blood plasma	Capsule filtrate	Urine
Proteins	7-9 parts per 100 parts of plasma	none	none
Urea	3 parts per 10000 parts of plasma	3 parts per 10000 parts of fluid.	2 parts per 100 parts of urine
Uric acid	3 parts per 100000 parts of plasma	3 parts per 100000 parts of fluid	5 parts per 10000 parts of urine
Ammonium Compounds	1 part per 100000 parts of plasma	1 part per 100000 parts of fluid	4 parts per 10000 parts of urine
Glucose	1 part per 1000 parts of plasma	1 part per 1000 parts of fluid	none

What do these facts tell you about the changes that take place in the capsule and the tubule?

Clearly the kidneys are concerned with more than just the removal of urine from the body. They regulate the loss of many other substances in addition to the nitrogen-containing waste substance urea: salts, amino acids and glucose, for example. In this way they help to control the composition of the blood and, indirectly, that of other body fluids. Urine is very largely water, but the quantity of water in the urine is much less than that which passes through the capsule wall into the tubules. Most of this water is re-absorbed through the wall of the loop of Henle into the capillary network enveloping it.

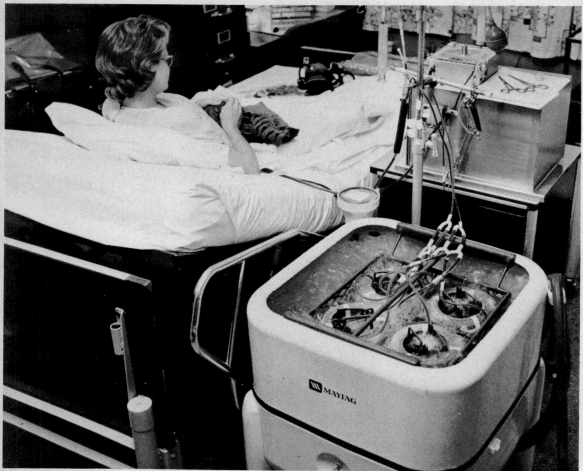

by courtesy of IPS

Fig 44. An artificial kidney machine

If the kidneys become diseased they may not function as effectively as they should so that poisonous waste materials collect in the tissues. This upsets the working of the tissues and causes swelling—*oedema*—due to the body retaining too much salt, water and other substances. Sometimes the kidneys fail to such an extent that an artificial kidney is used. This is able to remove water and waste substances and regulate the salt composition of the blood reducing the load on the diseased kidneys so that they have a better chance of recovering. Kidneys are also frequently transplanted.

The control of water loss from the kidneys is regulated by a hormone called *ADH* for short. It is released into the blood stream by the pituitary gland (see page 67). *ADH* reduces the loss of water but promotes the loss of certain salts.

6 The skin and heat loss

The skin: its structure and function

The skin is the outer covering of the body—a vital organ with a variety of important roles. Above all it acts as a protective barrier against bacteria and other organisms; it also acts as a cushion against injury. In this respect hair is also important. The skin has a rich supply of sense organs providing the brain with information about conditions in the surroundings. The skin also acts as a store for certain substances, notably fats. It is a waterproof barrier which prevents both the entry of water and its excessive loss. There is a rich blood supply to the skin which plays an important part in the regulation of heat loss and thus the body temperature. The skin contains sweat glands through which water containing salts and a little urea is passed from surrounding glands to the outside. It thus plays a small part in excretion and water loss.

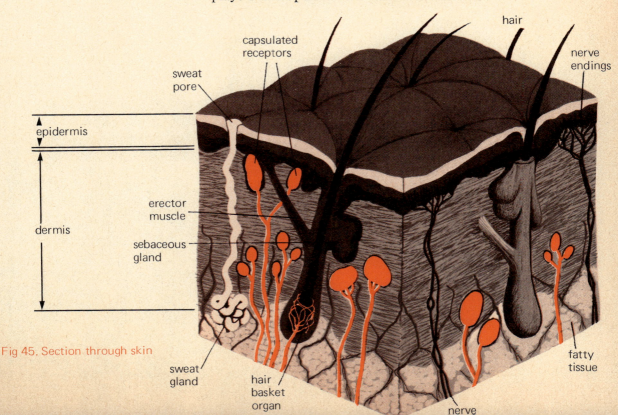

Fig 45. Section through skin

The area of skin in an adult human may be more than two square yards. Its structure is indicated in the block diagram. There are two main layers: an outer epidermis and an inner dermis. The outermost layer of the epidermis is a layer of dead cells which are eventually rubbed off. They form thick pads on the soles of the feet. The dead, outermost layer of the epidermis is derived from the inner layer called the *Malphighian layer* after Malpighi, the Italian microscopist who also first discovered capillaries. The cells of this layer divide frequently, and as more and more cells divide the older cells are gradually pushed to the surface where they eventually die. The Malphighian layer contains pigment which colours the skin. White skin exposed to the sun becomes brown due to the formation of more pigment which acts as a protection against the sunlight.

The dermis is largely composed of connective tissue. It contains nerve fibres and blood vessels which branch many times to form a dense capillary network. The epidermis has no nerves or blood vessels; this is important in the regulation of heat loss from the skin surface. In cold weather the capillaries contract and blood may be cut off altogether from some of them. The loss of heat is therefore reduced and the skin appears pallid. In hot weather the blood supply is increased, more blood is brought to the capillaries near the surface and more heat is lost, so helping to keep the body cool. At such times the skin appears flushed as in a fever. In cold weather we often develop a characteristic goose-pimpled appearance. This is due to the tiny muscle attached to each hair contracting. Furry animals are able to fluff up their fur to keep warm by such means. Air is trapped in the spaces between the hairs forming an insulating layer preventing excessive heat loss.

When the body gets hot we tend to sweat a lot. The *sweat* is a watery fluid released by the coiled *sweat glands* lying deep in the dermis, each with a straight duct passing to the skin surface, with an opening, the *sweat pore*. Sweat contains salt and some urea and other wastes. It is a minor form of excretion but, more important, the evaporation of the water from the skin surface causes cooling. Sweating is therefore an additional means of temperature regulation. It is under nervous control.

Hair is derived from the epidermis, though each hair root lies in a pit or *follicle* deep in the dermis. Only the skin of the palms and soles lacks hair follicles. The bottom of each follicle is like an egg cup upside down. Within the cup is the *papilla*, rich in blood capillaries. The hair is formed from a chain of hair cells which are horny and die. Pigment gives the

Fig 45b. Photomicrograph of human skin

Bryan Clarke: by courtesy of the Reed Engineering and Development Services Ltd hair its colour; grey hair is due to air trapped in the hair cells. Opening into the follicle is a gland, the *sebaceous gland*, which releases an oily secretion, *sebum*, which oils the hair and finds its way to the skin surface oiling and waterproofing the skin as well.

The base of the hair is surrounded by fine nerve fibres, forming the hair basket organ. The nerve endings are stimulated when the hair is touched. The other types of nerve ending in the skin are described in Chapter 8.

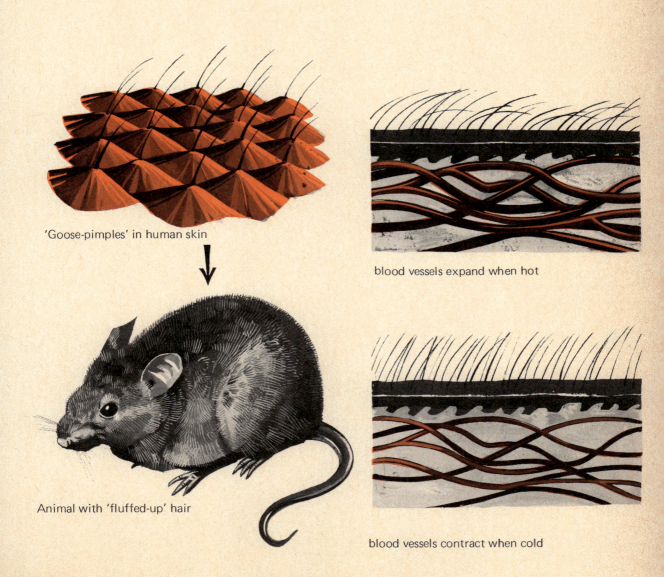

Fig 46. Diagram showing the effect of temperature on the skin

'Goose-pimples' in human skin

Animal with 'fluffed-up' hair

blood vessels expand when hot

blood vessels contract when cold

7 The skeleton and muscles

The role of the skeleton

The human skeleton is made mostly of a hard substance called *bone* with some softer, flexible material called *cartilage*. It provides a rigid framework supporting the softer body organs and other tissues. It is protective: the skull, for instance, contains and protects the brain; the rib cage contains and protects the lungs and heart. It serves for muscle attachment and, since it is jointed in parts and the muscles concerned with movements are arranged across joints, the bones act as levers for walking, bending, lifting objects etc. The skeleton gives a basic shape to the body and, although the shape of the body is not identical with that of the skeleton, by comparing the skeletons of different animals the connexion is readily observed.

Mammals living in water (eg. whales) have a comparatively light skeleton, their bodies being buoyed up by the water. Humans live on land and so require a fairly substantial skeleton for support and a well developed muscular system to provide movement and to maintain the upright posture which is one of our chief distinguishing characteristics. We have an inner skeleton or *endoskeleton*. (Many animals, such as insects, have a hard outer skeleton or *exoskeleton*). Our muscles are attached to the outside of the bones; an insect's are attached to the inside.

Fig 47.
The human skeleton and four types of joint
1. Sutures in skull
2. Sliding joint at ankle
3. Ball and Socket joint at Pelvis
4. Hinge joint at knee

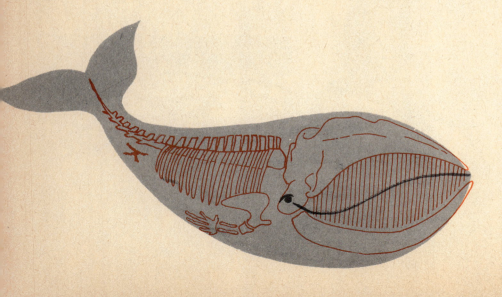

THE SKELETON AND MUSCLES 57

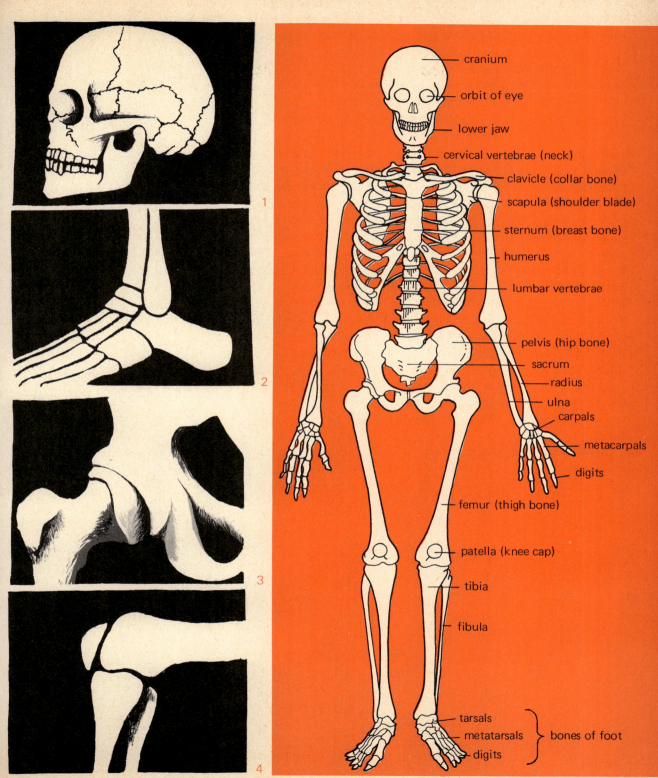

Fig 47.

The structure of the skeleton

The backbone, spine or *vertebral column* is the central jointed girder or axis of the skeleton. Attached to it are the skull, the rib cage, and the girdles: the hip or *pelvic* girdle bearing the leg bones and the shoulder or *pectoral* girdle bearing the bones of the arms. The places at which the bones come together are called *joints*. Joints are of various kinds, the type depending on the degree of movement and on the arrangement of the muscles and ligaments.

At joints where a fair degree of movement is required, the ends of the bones are smooth and separated by protective cartilages which act as shock absorbers. In the backbone, discs of cartilage between the vertebrae sometimes slip out of position, giving the painful condition of a slipped disc. There is sufficient movement between the vertebrae to allow bending of the trunk backwards, from side to side and forwards as in toe touching. But ball-and-socket joints such as at the hip and shoulder have a much greater range of movement, greater than a hinge joint such as the knee, or a sliding joint as in the ankle. The skull is made up of a number of bones which fit closely together, the joints between them being known as *sutures*. There is very little movement at a suture.

Look at the diagram of the various types of joint and assess the extent of movement at each. Move your fingers, arms, legs, etc., and see for yourself how the degree of movement varies.

Muscles are usually arranged across joints in pairs, one muscle moving the bone or bones in one direction and the other pulling it in the opposite direction. The diagram shows how the *triceps* and *biceps* muscles work together to bend the arm at the elbow and straighten it again.

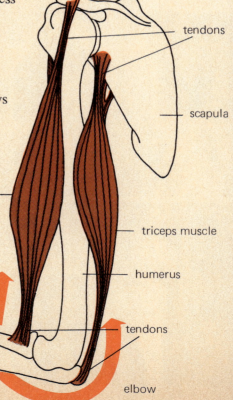

Fig 48. Shows the arrangement of muscles across a joint

Bones as levers

Bones act as levers moved by the action of muscles. Examples of the three main kinds of lever—first, second and third order—are to be found in the human body. The type depends on the relative positions of the pulling or lifting force, the point at which the lever is pivoted—its fulcrum—and the weight being lifted. The *mechanical advantage* of a lever is given by weight (load) divided by the force (effort). Because the pulling force usually acts closer to the fulcrum than the weight being lifted most muscles work at a mechanical disadvantage.

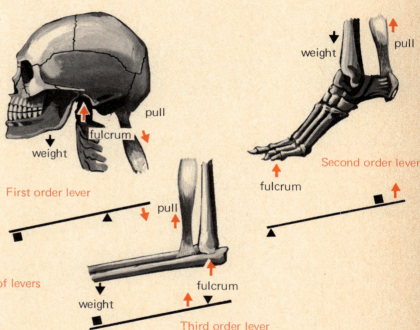

Fig 49. Shows the 3 orders of levers as applied to human joints

The construction of bones

Most people see bones at a butcher's shop and imagine them to be tough, solid, very hard, dead structures. This is only partly true, for bone is far from solid and in the body it is a living tissue with a rich supply of nerves and blood. The larger bones are hollow and filled with bone marrow and the bone substance itself is penetrated by a network of spaces, just as a bath sponge is.

The thigh bone or *femur* is a good example of a large hollow bone. Its upper third is stronger and of greater circumference than the lower part and it takes more strain. The hollow cavity economizes in bone substance and allows for a great saving in weight, so that muscles have less to move. This does not affect the strength of the bone for the

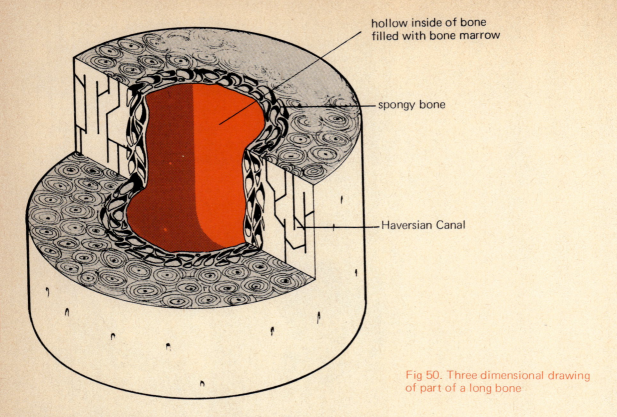

Fig 50. Three dimensional drawing of part of a long bone

outside of the bone is subjected to the greatest stress when a bending force is applied. This may be compared with the hollow frame of a bicycle or the way in which an engineer saves weight by using an 'H'-shaped girder in a structure such as a bridge instead of solid pieces of steel of square cross section. The point of attachment of muscles is also important so that too great a strain is not imposed on bones in their weakest points when muscles contract. Bones do break, of course. This will happen if a large force is applied in one place for a short time, for example, as in a bad fall. But bones are immensely strong and capable of withstanding strains considerably greater than those imposed by everyday activities—they have a high safety margin. A top weight lifter can lift over 400 lbs in weight, for instance, considerably in excess of his body weight.

Muscles and their action

When we run for a bus our leg muscles work rapidly, contracting (shortening) and relaxing (returning to their former length) to move our limbs. They receive larger quantities of fuel and oxygen in the blood in order to operate. Some of this energy source is converted to heat which is carried round the body in the bloodstream, so

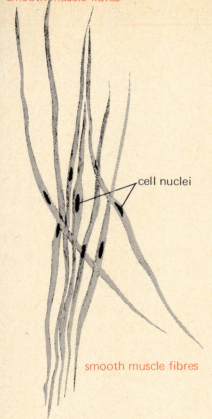

Fig 51. Highly magnified diagram of human striped muscle (below) and smooth muscle fibres

cell nuclei

smooth muscle fibres

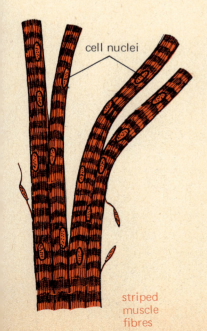

cell nuclei

striped muscle fibres

helping to maintain the high body temperature. Muscles, then, are not concerned solely with movement: they produce heat. In addition they can maintain a state of contraction to hold or fix parts of the body in place. They act like the guy ropes of a tent; the muscles holding parts of the body to maintain posture are examples.

The muscle of the heart pumps blood to the lungs and round the body when it contracts and the weak muscles in the walls of the larger veins contract to help blood back to the heart. Muscle in the wall of the gut helps to mix food and move it along. There are muscles in the ducts of glands, which regulate the outflow of fluid, and *sphincter* muscles at the intestine end of the stomach and at the anus control the movement of food out of the stomach and of food remains out of the body respectively. These are just a few of the ways in which muscles act.

The types of muscles
If we wish to move a finger or a leg we can consciously do so. The muscles involved are *voluntary* muscles. We have no conscious control of muscles in the gut wall; these are *involuntary* muscles. Under the microscope voluntary muscle tissue has a conspiciously striped appearance and so is also known as *striped* or *striated* muscle. Involuntary muscle, such as that of the gut, has no visible stripes and is called *smooth* or *unstriped* muscle. Heart muscle is a third kind of muscle tissue. Its fibres are branched, have some stripes and form an interlacing network ideal for the walls of a bag-shaped structure contracting throughout life many millions of times.

The fibres making up smooth and striped fibres are unbranched. Smooth muscle is able to contract relatively slowly but it can maintain a state of contraction for long periods. Striped muscle, on the other hand, can contract quickly but it also fatigues quickly. Try raising your arms at full stretch in front of you with a heavy book or similar object balanced on top of your hands. How long can you keep your arms horizontal?

Striped muscle contains muscle haemoglobin (*myoglobin*) which is able to store oxygen. This is almost certainly used in the burning of sugar to release energy for muscle contraction. Muscle performance—of voluntary muscles—can be improved with training. This is partly due to opening up of the blood supply to the tissue regularly in training so that greater supplies of fuel and oxygen can be brought to it, and this improved circulation also enables a much quicker removal of waste products, in addition to other biochemical changes.

8 The body's control systems

While sitting in a chair or on a stool pick up a needle from a table and thread some cotton through its eye. Think of the things you are doing from the time that you are asked to pick up the needle.

Your ears are receiving the sound of the person asking you to pick up the needle; your eyes will look for the needle and focus on it. Your arm will then be raised and your hand will move towards the needle with your fingers positioning themselves ready to pick it up. They will feel the needle and grasp it, your eyes, other arm and hand will then carry out a similar sequence of actions to pick up the cotton in order to place the end of the cotton through the needle's eye. Other actions may well be involved such as moving your head when looking for the needle and so on, but even when perfoming a simple series of actions such as those described, clearly a number of different parts of the body are used and they all work in a co-ordinated way so that you successfully perform the tasks that you set out to achieve.

We know that in the example quoted the ears, eyes, arm muscles, finger muscles and sense of touch, at least, are involved. The information that the ears receive must in some way result in the eyes moving in search of the needle and cotton and the subsequent orderly movements of the arm,

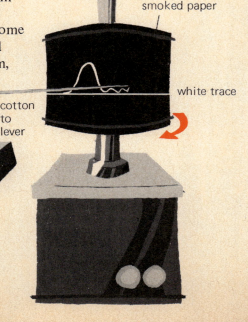

Fig 52. Producing a trace from a contracting gastrocnemius muscle

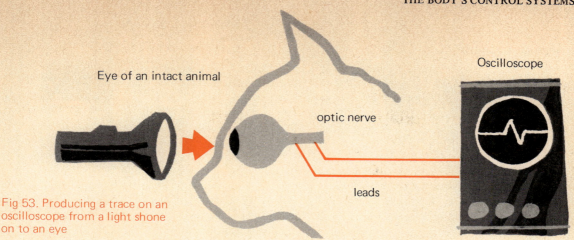

Fig 53. Producing a trace on an oscilloscope from a light shone on to an eye

fingers etc. How are the parts coordinated? How is information received, interpreted and passed on to other parts for them to act in the appropriate way?

We know that if the thigh or *gastrocnemius muscle* with its nerve attached is removed from a freshly killed frog, is kept moist, and the nerve given a small electric shock then the muscle will contract. Perhaps the electric current has passed along the nerve causing the muscle to contract, but it is possible to measure the speed with which the message passing from nerve to muscle travels and this is much lower than the high speed of an electric current. A nerve can also be stimulated by other means, such as dropping a small drop of acid onto it. Clearly something—a message or impulse—passes along the nerve to the muscle causing the latter to contract. It is possible to connect the optic nerve (the nerve linking the eye to the brain) of a frog or a cat to an oscilloscope which indicates on its screen any electrical signal. If a light is flashed in the eye a trace appears on the oscilloscope screen for the time that the eye is exposed to the light flash. If the optic nerve to that eye is cut or blocked using extreme cold and the light is then flashed on no trace appears on the oscilloscope. No impulse passes along the optic nerve. The eye must contain cells which are sensitive to light and signals pass from these to the brain along the optic nerve, if the nerve is intact.

If a blow is aimed at your face you will automatically move your head out of the way or raise your hands in self defence. The movement of the oncoming blow affects the pattern of light reaching your eyes and signals pass from them to the brain along the optic nerve. If the nerves to the arm or head muscles were linked to an oscilloscope, then traces would be obtained as with the frog thigh muscle showing that impulses were passing from the brain to the muscle, the brain having received impulses from the eyes.

The nervous system

receive information from the surroundings—they are called *receptors*—and are linked to the central nervous system by nerves. The central nervous system is linked in turn with organs such as muscles, which carry out or effect actions as the result of receiving nervous impulses—these are called *effectors.* Nerves linking receptors to the central nervous system are called *sensory nerves* and those linking the central nervous system to effectors are called *motor nerves.* Nerve fibres of a third type link one part of the central nervous system to another.

The diagram shows the central nervous system and the major peripheral nerves. In addition to the central nervous system and the nerves linking muscles and the external sense organs, the body has another system of nerves controlling its inner workings. This system works automatically and is known as the *autonomic nervous system.* It supplies the gut, blood vessels and heart, kidneys, lungs, bladder, the iris muscles of the eyes, and other internal organs. It is concerned with such largely automatic procedures as the rate of heartbeat and breathing, the diameter of the blood vessels, the size of the pupils of the eyes and the movement of food through the gut. It is, of course, intimately connected with the central nervous system, and if an arm muscle is used extensively, for example, then there will be corresponding changes in the blood supply to the muscle so that increased quantities of fuel and oxygen are carried to it and waste materials removed effectively.

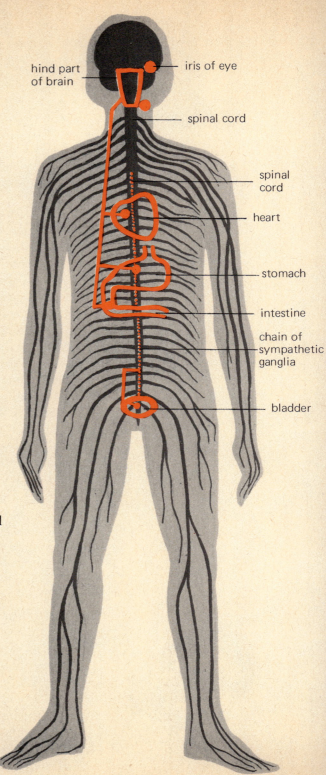

Fig 54. Diagram showing autonomic and peripheral nervous systems in man, greatly simplified

— peripheral nerve
— autonomic nerve

THE BODY'S CONTROL SYSTEMS 65

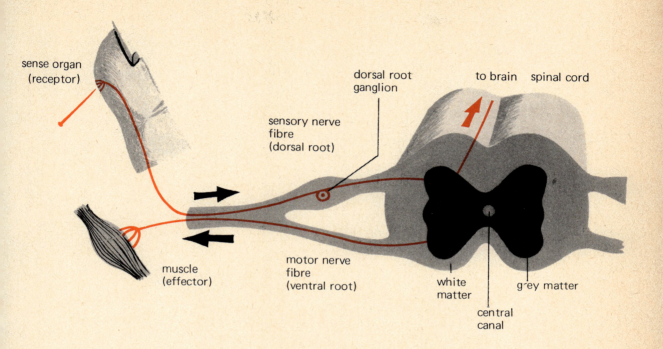

Fig 55. The reflex arc showing the path followed by the nerve impulse, in this case between a sense organ in a finger and a muscle in the arm

The reflex arc
If a sense organ, for example a pain receptor, is stimulated, a signal will pass from it along a sensory nerve fibre to the spinal cord. Another signal travels out from the spinal cord to an effector organ, in this instance an arm muscle, along a motor nerve. The effector organ acts in the appropriate way: if it is a muscle it will contract. The pathway that the nerve signals follow is called a *reflex arc*.

Chemical messengers
A person whose limbs are paralysed may have lost the ability to walk—to use the leg muscles—and the sense of feeling, but the limbs continue to function in other ways although the nerve supply is not working. Clearly then the nervous system does not work alone in controlling the body's various activities. What other system do you think might be able to carry signals of some kind? Consider the following facts as they are described for developing blowfly maggots (larvae).

If several blowfly larvae, which have moulted for the last time, are ligatured, as illustrated, the hind part of each does not develop into a pupa but the front part does.

Untreated maggots pupate as usual.

Maggots which are just about to pupate when ligatured still pupate as usual.

The ligatures should be tied behind the brain each time so that the central nervous system is not damaged. The hind ends of the maggots move despite the ligatures showing that the nerves from the brain are undamaged.

What do these facts tell you? Where is the signal produced and how might it be carried? If the nervous system is not damaged which other system might carry signals and what form might these signals take?

unligatured maggot

maggot ligatured when young

maggot ligatured when older

Fig 56. Effects of ligaturing blowfly maggots at different ages

Hormones

The nervous system does not work alone in controlling the body's various activities. In addition to control by nerves a chemical control system is in operation. The chemicals, called *hormones,* are produced by *ductless* or *endocrine* glands whose products are released into the bloodstream— not along ducts—and so carried to all parts of the body. Nerve signals reach only the part supplied by each fibre. Although hormones are

Fig 57. Diagram showing location of endocrine glands (both male and female)

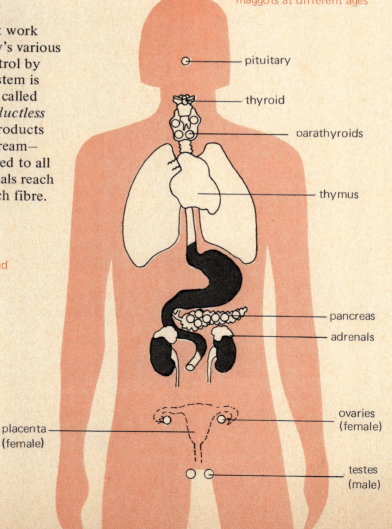

distributed everywhere in the bloodstream, they do not necessarily act on every tissue. A hormone may act on a specific gland or part of that gland. The pituitary gland produces several such hormones: one, known as ACTH for short, acts on the cortex of the adrenal glands; the growth hormone produced by the thyroid, on the other hand, acts generally on the body tissue.

But, whatever the roles of each hormone, their success—as with any system employing signals—depends on the appropriate tissue making the same response each time. For instance, when the pituitary releases a hormone acting on the thyroid, the thyroid gland will produce more growth hormone. There is, of course, a reciprocal arrangement in which the level of growth hormone will affect the amount of hormone that the pituitary is producing. A high level of growth hormone, for instance, will result in the production of less hormone by the pituitary and vice versa. The levels of hormones in the blood reaching the tissues are thus continually fluctuating to produce an over-all 'balance' of body activities.

Nerves are concerned with immediate action—a muscle or gland is instructed to act in a certain way in an instant. Chemical signals can act very quickly—as in the release of adrenalin into the bloodstream to produce increased heartbeat rate, preparing the body for fighting or fleeing action when a potentially dangerous situation is encountered. Generally speaking, the *endocrine system* is concerned with the long-term control of body activities: control of growth, the repair and replacement of body tissues, the development and function of sex organs, and the day-to-day control of blood sugar level.

The main organs producing hormones are the *pituitary*—sometimes called the master gland because it produces many hormones which altogether have many actions—the *thyroid, pancreas, adrenals, parathyroids,* and the reproductive organs: *ovaries* and *testes,* and the *placenta* in pregnancy. The *thymus* gland is also important during development but gradually degenerates. The table summarizes the main hormones and their action.

Our knowledge of the endocrine glands, the hormones they produce, and their action has largely been obtained by means of experiments on animals, later supported by the work of doctors in hospitals. Dogs, rats, rabbits, mice, monkeys and pigs have been used—all are mammals having a similar physiology to man's.

Gland	Hormone	Action
Pituitary -anterior	Growth hormone	Affects growth of all cells. Too much hormone causes gigantism, too little produces a pituitary dwarf.
	Thyrotropic hormone	Acts on thyroid causing it to release thyroid hormone.
	Prolactin	Causes mammary glands to produce milk.
	ACTH (adrenocorticotropic hormone)	Causes adrenal cortex to release its hormones.
	Sex hormones (2)	One causes ovaries to produce eggs and testes to manufacture sperms. A second causes thickening of womb lining ready to receive a fetilized egg and growth of the placenta during pregnancy.
-posterior	Oxytocin	Causes womb to contract and expel the child during 'labour' and increased milk production.
	Vasopressin (ADH)	Controls water and salt loss from kidneys in the urine.
Thyroid	Thyroxine Triiodothyronine	Increases cell chemical reactions so affecting growth. Too little hormone in childhood causes cretinism: the child is physically and mentally backward. In adults too little causes weight increase, puffiness, thickening of skin, course and brittle hair, slow mental and physical actions and lethargic state results (myxoedema). Lack of iodine in the diet causes gland to enlarge (exophthalmic goitre).

Adrenals
  -medulla
  (central part)
	Adrenalin	Prepares body for action by increasing heartbeat and blood supply to muscles but reducing it to gut and skin as during sudden fright, for instance. Blood sugar released from liver to supply more fuel.

-cortex (outer part)	Group of hormones called steroids	Prepare body to meet long-term stress conditions (pregnancy, illness etc). Exact action not known but appear to be concerned with cell respiration and energy production. Steroid production is stimulated by ACTH of pituitary.
Pancreas	Insulin	Acts on cells enabling them to use glucose for providing energy; so controls blood sugar level. Underproduction of insulin results in too high blood sugar level and appearance of sugar in urine-sugar diabetes or diabetes mellitus. Overproduction depletes blood sugar to abnormally low level-as serious a condition as diabetes.
	Glucagon	Discovered recently. Exact role not known but opposite action to insulin (in this respect similar to adrenalin).
Parathyroids	PTH (parathyroid hormone)	Connected with calcium metabolism, increasing its uptake through intestine. Removal causes tetany-continued contraction of muscles.
Reproductive organs (testes, ovaries and placenta)	Several	Control of sexual maturity, secondary sexual characteristics (hair growth, mammary glands, etc) and activities such as menstrual cycle, pregnancy and production of milk by mammary glands.
Thymus	Thymus hormone	Recently discovered, thought to control the development of immunity. Manufactures lymphocytes.

Insulin: its discovery and development

The story of the discovery of insulin by Frederick Banting and Charles Best, and their early work on its action is a classic example of experimental work. It is presented here in problem form. Look at the evidence and try to answer the questions.

In 1889 Minkowski and von Mering removed the pancreas from several dogs. This resulted in the dogs having a high blood sugar level and the appearance of sugar in the dog's urine-the condition of *diabetes mellitus*.

What does this suggest? and What control experiment would you have carried out to support this?

In subsequent experiments dogs were operated on without the removal of the pancreas and diabetes was not produced.

What does this show?

Unsuccessful attempts were made to relieve diabetes by injecting pancreas extracts. Banting realized that the pancreas produces digestive enzymes and that if the gland produced a hormone then it might be destroyed by these. This might be the reason why the pancreas extracts failed to relieve diabetes. Certain parts of the pancreas-the *Islets of Langerhans*-were known often to be degenerated in diabetic patients.

What does this last fact suggest?

Banting was eventually able to produce an active extract from the pancreas, the digestive ducts of which had been ligatured so that the enzyme-producing tissue degenerated and only the hormone-producing tissue remained healthy. With this extract he succeeded in reducing high blood sugar levels in diabetic dogs. Sugar was also injected into dogs to produce artificially high blood sugar level. Injections of extract reduced the level to normal. Over-injection of extract even produced low blood sugar levels.

What do these facts suggest?

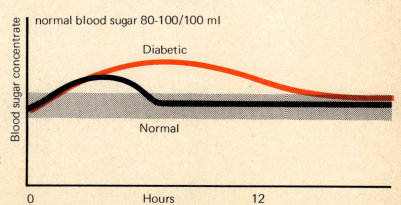

When given a dose of sugar (see time 0) a normal person burns it up quickly, but a diabetic takes much longer.

Banting and Best first named the substance in the extract, which was responsible for reducing high blood sugar levels, *isletin*, and it later became known as *insulin*.

Banting was next able to prepare an active preparation from whole pancreas by immersing the pancreas in acid alcohol solution. He found out the strength of each quantity of extract by observing how much it lowered blood sugar level and having prepared an even purer preparation from ox pancreas in 1922 this was injected into an eleven-year-old diabetic boy, Leonard Thompson, in a Toronto Hospital. The symptoms of diabetes were relieved after a number of injections.

What did this confirm?

Today insulin is prepared in very pure forms and the giving of injections is a routine procedure. Even a young child can give himself regular daily injections. Ultimately it is hoped that all diabetics will be able to take a special form of insulin by mouth. A diabetic has to take injections for life. Giving a diabetic doses of insulin every day will not help his pancreas to produce any more insulin.

The Senses

If someone throws a ball to you, or at you, you will either endeavour to catch it or duck out of the way. If you touch something hot you will feel heat—perhaps pain as well. If a needle point is placed very lightly on the skin then you will merely feel light pressure. You are able to see light with your eyes, to hear sound with your ears, and to taste and smell substances. The body is equipped with the means of receiving and reacting to outside influences or *stimuli*. Our survival is dependent on the right responses being made to them.

The skin
The outer protective covering of the body, the skin, has a rich supply of receptors and so is able to respond to changes in the surroundings with which it is in contact. From the information that the central nervous system receives from skin receptors we are able to decide whether the 'thing' with which we are in contact is pleasant or unpleasant, desirable or undesirable, something to go towards or something to go away from to avoid injury. The lips, soles of the feet, and palms are especially sensitive areas.

Various types of nerve ending in the skin are receptive to temperature, pressure, or pain. Within the body, too, are different kinds of receptor. For instance, the absence of food in the gut for a long time produces the sensation of hunger. A stone blocking the bile duct will cause pain and so will a stomach ulcer.

Taste and smell

Receptors are mostly on the tongue, but also on the roof of the mouth and the back of the throat. Like the smell receptors in the lining of the roof of the nose they are sensitive to chemicals. Together, the taste and smell receptors sample chemicals in the surroundings—in food, air and so on.

The taste receptors, *taste buds,* are flask-shaped structures arranged on small projections scattered over the surface of the tongue. They are linked with nerve fibres, and when a chemical comes into contact with the sensitive cells signals pass along the nerve fibres to the central nervous system according to the kind of chemical present. The smell receptors work in a similar way, and, like the taste bud cells, are kept moist by fluid released by special gland cells. Chemicals pass into solution, before the taste and smell cells are stimulated.

If you place different substances on the tongue you will discover which parts are more sensitive to them. Sugar, salt, lemon juice and other easily obtained substances with characteristic tastes are suitable. The tip is more sensitive to sweet and salty substances, the sides to acid and the back part to bitter substances.

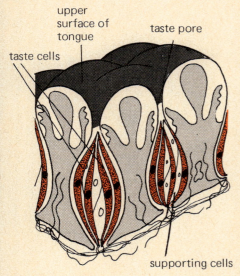

Fig 59a. Block diagram showing taste receptors in human tongue

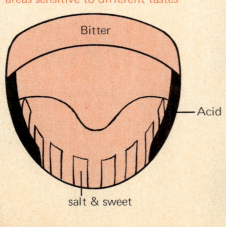

Fig 59b. Map of tongue showing areas sensitive to different tastes

72 HUMAN BIOLOGY

The eye and sight

The eyes are receptive to light. They are normally only sensitive to 'visible' light. They cannot detect ultra-violet light as some insects can. Along with heat receptors in the skin they are the only receptors we have that are sensitive to radiation.

We have two eyes in the front of the head, held in sockets in the skull. Each eye is a sphere filled with fluid which maintains its shape. The wall of the sphere has three main layers: a tough outer layer called the *sclera* visible at the front as the white of the eye; a coloured middle layer containing blood vessels, the *choroid*, which forms the blue or brown part (iris) at the front of the eye; and, on the inside, the *retina* which contains light-sensitive cells. The central area of the sclera at the front is transparent and forms the *cornea*.

The outer edge of the iris is called the *ciliary body*. It is a thickened band of tissue containing muscle and its action is to alter the shape of the lens and thus change its focal length.

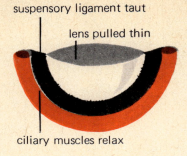

suspensory ligament taut
lens pulled thin
ciliary muscles relax

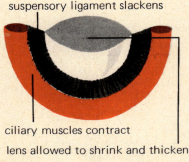

suspensory ligament slackens
ciliary muscles contract
lens allowed to shrink and thicken

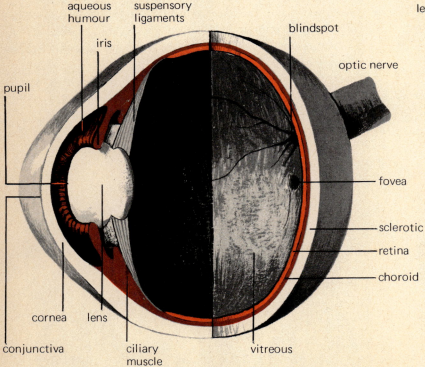

Fig 60. Diagram of human eye cut away to show its structure

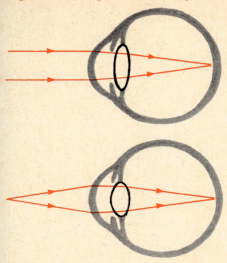

Fig 61a. Focusing on a distant object

Fig 61b. Focusing on a near object

The *lens* is suspended from the ciliary body by the *suspensory ligament*. Between the lens and the cornea the eye is filled with a watery fluid, the *aqueous humour*. The space between the lens and the back of the eye contains a more jelly-like *vitreous humour*.

The front of the eye is covered with a thin, transparent protective layer, which is called the *conjuctiva*. In the condition of 'pink eye' it becomes inflamed; this is called *conjunctivitis*. Adjacent to the eyeball are the tear glands. Fluid (tears) from these is wiped over the front of the eyeball by the eyelids each time they blink. The tear fluid helps protect the cornea in washing away dust particles and also moistens and nourishes it. This is necessary because the cornea has no blood supply.

Each eye is held and moved in its socket by the action of six eye muscles whose action is co-ordinated so that both eyes usually move together.

The eye and light

Light rays entering the eye are bent considerably by the cornea and a little more by the lens, which acts as the fine adjustment to focus the rays on the retina at the back of the eye. The hole in the middle of the iris can open and close, like the diaphragm of a camera, to allow more or less light to enter the eye and fall on the delicate light-sensitive cells of the retina. These are easily damaged by very strong light.

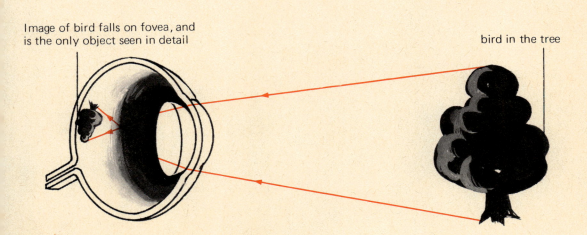

Image of bird falls on fovea, and is the only object seen in detail

bird in the tree

Fig 62. Diagram to show image formation in the eye by the cornea and the lens

When you look into somebody's eyes, the hole in the iris looks like a dark spot. This hole is called the pupil.

Because the lens is flexible its shape can be altered by the actions of the ciliary muscles so that both near and distant things can be focused onto the retina. When the ciliary muscles contract, so resisting the tension exerted by the sclera, the suspensory ligament relaxes allowing the lens to become fatter: in this way close objects are brought into focus. To bring distant objects into focus the ciliary muscles relax and the pull of the sclera puts tension on the suspensory ligament so that the lens becomes thinner and flatter.

The retina
The two main types of cell sensitive to light in the retina are called *rods* and *cones.* One part of the retina at the back of the eye, a shallow depression where light is brought to a focus, contains most of the cones; it is called the *yellow spot* or *fovea centralis.* The cones are sensitive to bright light and colour and it is in the fovea where the sharpest picture is received because the cone cells are close together. The rods are sensitive to dim light and do not perceive colour. This is why colours seem to disappear at dusk and we see only in greys and silver in moonlight.

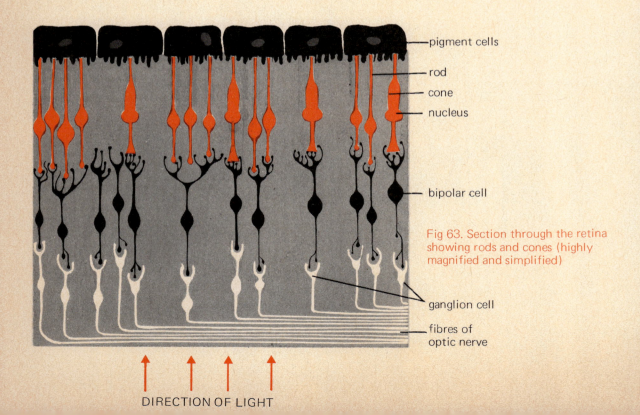

Fig 63. Section through the retina showing rods and cones (highly magnified and simplified)

THE BODY'S CONTROL SYSTEMS 75

left eye closed

both eyes open

right eye closed

Fig 64. Stereoscopic vision

Each rod and cone cell is linked to a nerve fibre. The nerve fibres are arranged over the surface of the retina and join up to form the optic nerve. They leave the eye near the fovea at the back of the eye and at this point there are no light sensitive cells. It is called the *blind spot*.

We have already said that both our eyes are in the front of the head. We see almost the same things with both eyes and so our vision is said to be binocular. Because the fields of vision of our two eyes overlap we see a three-dimensional picture.

Defects of the eye

Most people have an eye defect during their life. Most of these defects if not present in us when younger, will develop as we get older and are the result of lens defects. Defects of this type can largely be corrected by the use of spectacles. Some people can see near objects perfectly well but are unable to focus on distant objects; they are said to be *short sighted*. This is because light rays from a distant object are brought to a focus in front of the retina. The lenses in a pair of spectacles must be so arranged, therefore, that they spread the light before it enters the eye. Short sight is generally due to the lens being too fat, but also because the eyeball may be too long.

When the eye can focus on distant objects, but not near objects, it is said to be *long sighted*. For reading or looking at close objects spectacles with converging lenses are worn. Rays from a close object are brought to focus beyond the retina. Converging lenses help the eye lens to gather the light rays so that they are brought to a focus on the retina. Long sight may be due to a short eyeball or to a lens being flatter than usual. As people age there is a natural tendency for the lens to become harder and less elastic and the ciliary muscles may be weaker and so less able to resist the pull of the sclera. *Accommodation,* the ability of the eye to focus, becomes more difficult. There is a natural tendency for the power of accommodation to be reduced.

Fig 65. Correction for long sight

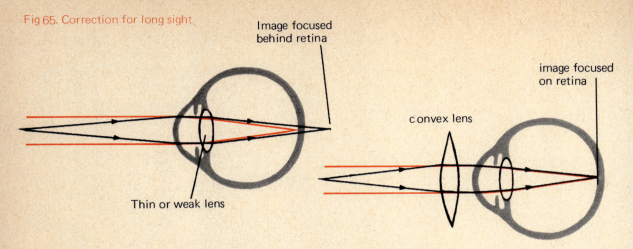

Fig 65 (b). Correction for short sight

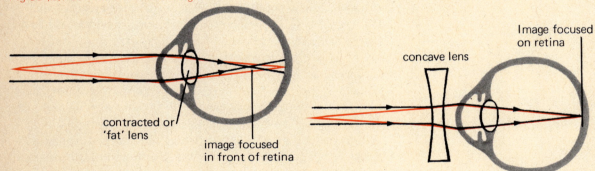

Astigmatism is a common defect; the eye is unable to focus on horizontal and vertical lines at the same time, because the surface of the lens is not equally curved. Cylindrical lenses which bend light more in the direction required are used for spectacles to correct this defect.

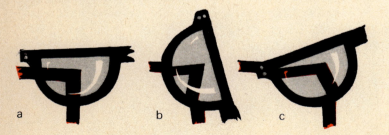

If you tilt your glasses when looking at a square corner and it looks like (b) or (c) you suffer from astigmatism

Fig 66. Astigmatism

If you shut one eye and look at this picture and some lines look darker, you suffer from astigmatism

The ear: organ of hearing and balance

When the string of a musical instrument is plucked it vibrates, causing the surrounding air to vibrate. The sound spreads outwards in all directions as more and more air vibrates. If the vibrations reach our ears they pass into the ear apparatus and make the eardrum vibrate; this is 'felt' by sensitive cells and a signal passes from these cells along nerve fibres to the brain which interprets them as sound. Sound waves can only travel through something which can vibrate, for example, gases, liquids, solids. It cannot travel through a vacuum because there is nothing to vibrate.

In addition to receiving sound waves, the ear has parts which are concerned with balance.

The ear and hearing.
The illustration shows the structure of the ear and the path of sound waves through it to the cells which are sensitive to vibrations. The ear consists of three main parts, the *outer*, *middle* and *inner* ears.

The ear flap or *pinna* collects sound waves and they are funnelled along the *ear passage* to the ear drum (*tympanic membrane*) which borders the outer ear and the middle ear. The middle ear is an air-filled cavity across which is the chain of ear bones: hammer (*malleus*), anvil (*incus*) and stirrup (*stapes*) joined at one end to the ear drum by the malleus and at the other to another membrane (*oval window*) by the stapes. Vibration of the air in the ear passage causes the ear

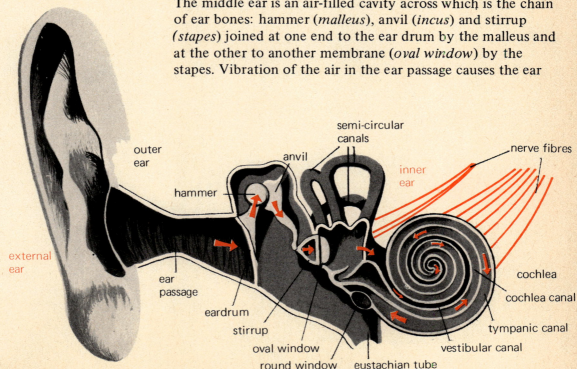

Fig 67. A section through the human ear

drum to vibrate and its movements vibrate the ear bones which push and pull the oval window stretched across a hole in the bony wall of the middle ear.

Within the bone beyond the oval window is a fluid-filled system of sacs and canals. Some are concerned with balance but a long, coiled tube, the *cochlea*, is concerned with hearing. Movement of the fluid within the cochlea affects tiny, sensitive hair cells which have a nerve supply. Movement of the hairs causes nerve signals to pass along the nerve fibres to the brain where they are translated into sound. The brain 'hears', not the ear itself.

The range of sounds that we can hear varies from person to person, but generally covers a range from about 15 cycles per second (a very low note) up to about 20,000 cycles per second, a note much higher than the highest note on the piano. Animals such as dogs have a greater range and bats, which use a direction-finding system employing squeaks, emit sounds which are much too high for the human ear to detect. We hear only the lowest notes emitted.

The air-filled middle ear is connected to the back of the throat by the *eustachian tube*. This is opened when we swallow or cough and the air pressure on either side of the ear drum is then equalized. The pressure may build up quickly as when in an aircraft that loses height quickly when coming into land, or even in a car travelling fast down a steep hill. If you swallow—sucking a boiled sweet is recommended—this helps to relieve any discomfort. Catarrh from a very heavy cold may also block the eustachian tube.

Another safety device is the arrangement of two muscles in the middle ear, one joined to the ear drum and the other to the stapes. When extremely loud sounds are received the muscles shorten automatically, tautening the ear drum and oval window and so cutting down their to and fro movement.

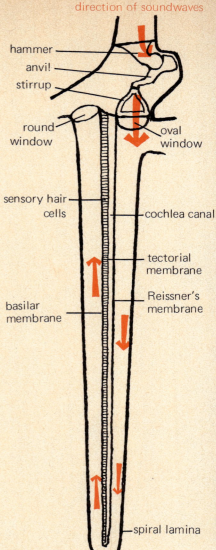

Fig 68. Diagram of cochlea unwound

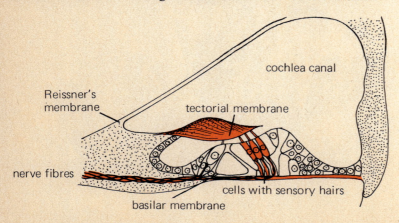

Fig 69. Section through cochlea canal

The cochlea

If the coiled tube of the cochlea is unravelled it can be seen as a tapering tube made up of three canals, each filled with fluid. The upper, outer canal has at its base the oval window, the lower canal is in contact with the round window. These two outer canals are connected with each other in the top of the cochlea through a tiny opening. When the oval window vibrates pressure waves travel through the fluid to the round window. The outer canals are separated by the cochlea canal and a band of tissue, the *spiral lamina*, containing sensitive hair cells attached to a thin strip of tissue, the *basilar membrane*. Fibres are arranged across this along its length, short ones at the broad end of the cochlea gradually increasing in length as the cochlea narrows. A short piano string gives a high note when struck, a long one a low note. It is thought that the short fibres respond to the high notes and the long ones to the low notes so that the lowest notes are received at the tip of the cochlea and the highest at the base.

Balance. Joined to the cochlea is the system of sacs and canals concerned with balance. There are three *semi-circular canals* branching off a large sac, the *utricle*, which is connected with another sac, the *saccule*. Within one end of each canal where it is swollen is a thickened ridge of tissue, called a *crista*, containing sensitive cells. The hairs project into a mass of

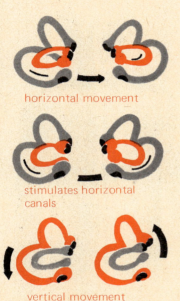

Fig 70. Balance and the semi-circular canals

horizontal movement

stimulates horizontal canals

vertical movement stimulates vertical canals

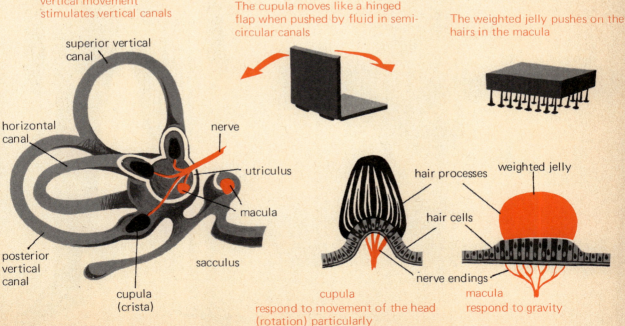

jelly, and when the head is moved the corresponding movement of the fluid in the canals pushes the flap of jelly so stimulating the hair cells. These are connected to nerve fibres which convey the nerve signals produced to the brain. The brain is also receiving information continuously from other parts of the body—the eyes, and neck, leg, feet and back muscles—which together with the signals from the balance organs in the ears are used in keeping us in the position we want to be.

Because the semi-circular canals are arranged at right angles to each other movement in any direction will stimulate at least one of the cristae. The saccule and utricle also each contain sensitive regions called *maculae* which are arranged at right angles to each other and attached to a side wall of each chamber. Weighted jelly presses down continuously on the hair cells so that changes in the position of the head will affect the force that the jelly exerts on the hair cells, and the pattern of nerve signals passing to the brain will be changed. Space pilots working in the weightless conditions of space have special problems to overcome in maintaining their balance, for on earth the receptors concerned are working in relation to the force of gravity. The signals that the brain receives from the various balance receptors will have different relative importance.

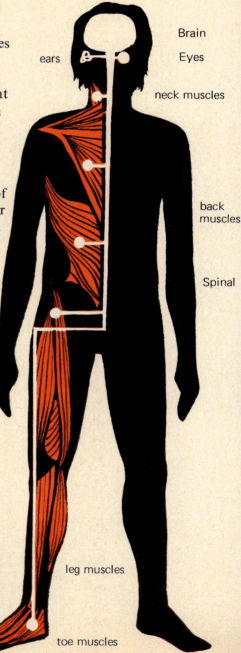

Fig 71. Parts of the human body concerned with balance (simplified)

Fig 72. Weightless condition

Much of the body's control of balance is automatic. When standing up, for instance, we do not think consciously where the various parts of our body are, but the brain can over-rule the automatic control system when we wish to change the position that we are in.

Practical problems

1. Place a ticking watch at various points round the blindfolded subject at equal distances from him as indicated. Does he guess the positions of the watch more accurately in certain places?
2. Plug the right ear and move the watch around as before. Repeat with just the left ear plugged. Is there any difference in the subject's ability to guess the positions of the watch?
3. Blindfold a subject and hold a ticking watch near one ear and move it slowly. Record the distance when the sound of the watch can no longer be heard. Repeat with other members of the class and record the distance for each person. Make a histogram indicating the numbers that occur in given distance regions.
4. Spin round and round rapidly several times whilst standing. What happens when you stop turning and why is this?
5. Mark a black spot and a cross 2½ inches apart on a piece of white card as shown. Hold up card in front of you about 18 inches away and with your left eye closed. While looking at the black spot with your right eye bring the card towards the face slowly. You will see the cross out of the corner of your eye. What happens to the cross as the card is moved closer towards the eye and why?.

9 Reproduction

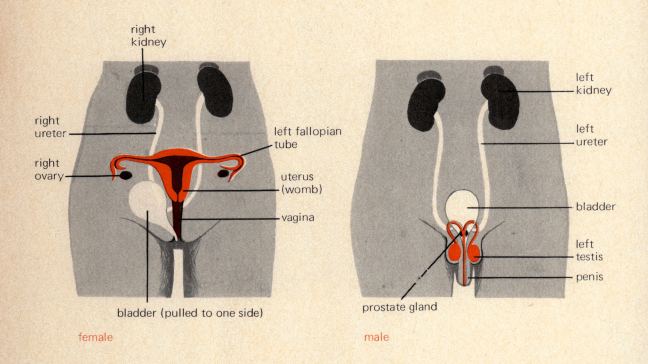

Fig 73. Human reproductive systems shown diagrammatically

In humans, as in other mammals, reproduction is by sexual means; that is, it involves sex cells. A female sex cell (*egg*) is fertilized by a male sex cell (*sperm*) and the fertilized egg or *zygote* develops eventually into a sexually mature human capable of reproducing.

The human reproductive system

The human reproductive system is designed so that the egg produced within the body of the female is fertilized there and develops there for a lengthy period—usually nine months. During this time the developing child is nourished and protected by an elaborate structure, the *placenta*. This forms from the greatly thickened lining of the mother's womb (*uterus*) and from part of the embryo (the growing fertilized egg). The tissues of the embryo and mother are in very close contact, therefore, enabling efficient exchange of food, oxygen and waste substances.

The diagrams show the basic structure of the human reproductive system and the excretory system with which it is closely associated. Sperms are produced by the two *testes* which consist of masses of coiled tubes. The sperms are introduced into the *uterus* by the insertion of the tubular *penis* into the *vagina*. The penis becomes erect due to the increased flow of blood into it and gland cells in the walls of the vagina release a lubricating fluid to aid the entry of the penis into the vagina. Stimulation of sensitive cells in the tip of the penis results in the release of *semen* containing sperms—semen is a complex fluid produced by the testes and various glands (e.g. the prostate gland).

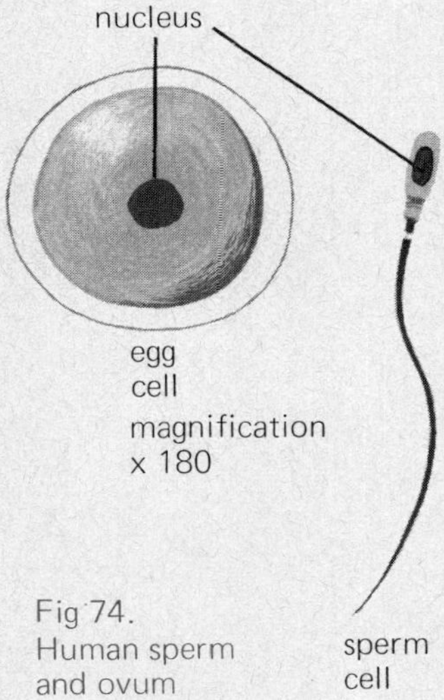

Fertilization

The sperms are able to swim in the fluid using lashing movements of their tails and enter the uterus. Their passage through the uterus and into the *fallopian tubes* (egg ducts) may be aided by movements of these structures and if an egg cell is on its way down the fallopian tube the sperms will be chemically attracted to it. Fertilization usually occurs high up in the fallopian tubes: it is the penetration of the egg cell by a sperm cell and the fusion of the egg cell nucleus with that of the sperm.

On average about 300,000 sperms are released at a time, but generally not more than one enters an egg. If two enter the egg then twin embryos are produced resulting in identical twins. Occasionally two eggs are released at the same time and twins will also result if both are fertilized. They will not in this case be identical.

Generally eggs are released one at a time each month (28 days) by alternate ovaries—each ovary releases an egg every two months.

Whilst the egg is developing in the ovary changes are taking place in the uterus so that, if, following the egg's release, it is fertilized, the uterus is fully prepared to receive it. As the uterus lining thickens, blood vessels and glands increase and there is greater muscle development. If fertilization fails to occur the lining continues to thicken for another fourteen days or so before it breaks down with characteristic loss of blood. This erosion of the uterus lining with bleeding is called *menstruation* —popularly known as a period.

There is a close link between the cycle of events in which the uterus lining thickens and then breaks down—the *menstrual cycle*—and the changes that take place in the ovaries in the

Fig 74.
Human sperm and ovum

nucleus
egg cell
magnification x 180
sperm cell

formation and release of an egg cell—the *oestrus cycle*. Both cycles are under the control of the hormonal system though emotional factors can influence and upset the normal rhythm.

The average menstrual cycle is about 28 days although 26-30 day cycles are common and shorter and longer cycles are known to occur. Bleeding usually lasts from four to six days with a blood loss of some 30-40 ml. The first *menses*, or flow of blood, starts at about the age of twelve, sometimes earlier, and may go on each month until a woman is about 45-50 years old. At this time the 'change' occurs; menstruation gradually gets less frequent, finally stopping altogether.

Women who take the 'pill' have a cycle whose length is controlled artificially. Ovulation does not occur but menstruation does take place.

The egg cycle and menstrual cycle are usually interrupted only if a pregnancy ensues. After the birth of the child the

Fig 75. Diagram showing sequence of typical menstrual cycle. The numbers are days in the cycle

after a few days

four weeks

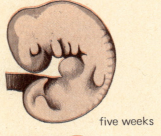
five weeks

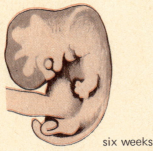
six weeks

menstrual cycle starts once more and menstruation normally occurs a few weeks afterwards. If the baby is breastfed this will delay the onset of menstruation.

Pregnancy

The fertilized egg cell, containing one set of *chromosomes* (see page 90) contributed by the egg and another from the sperm (23 from each making the normal body cell number of 46), soon starts to divide and, by the time it reaches the uterus and actually becomes embedded or *implanted* in the thickened uterus lining, it has divided many times to produce a sphere containing a mass of cells inside it. Most of the inner cell mass forms the growing embryo and a little of it, together with the hollow sphere wall and the uterus lining adjacent, grows to form the placenta.

The parts of the foetus become distinct fairly quickly (see diagrams), so that at twelve weeks it is recognizably human. The changes in the remaining 28 weeks are mostly internal ones especially the great development and refinement of the nervous system. During its period in the womb—the *gestation period* lasting about 280 days—the growing foetus is protected by a fluid-filled sac. This bursts just prior to the birth process and the foetus is then expelled from the womb by the automatic muscular contractions of the uterus wall. This is known as 'labour'. The umbilical cord connecting mother and child, and which for most of the pregnancy has been the route along which food and oxygen and waste are exchanged, has to be tied and cut. The newly born child is then reliant on its own lungs for

seven weeks

three months

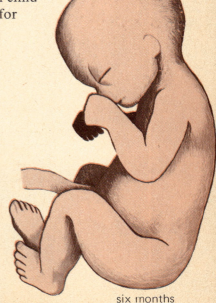
six months

Figure 76. Some stages in the development of the human embryo

attaining sufficient oxygen and removing carbon dioxide waste, on its excretory system for removing urine, and on its other organs for carrying out other vital functions.

The breastfed child will receive its nourishment from the milk produced by the mother's breasts or *mammary glands*. Under the influence of hormones, produced first by a structure in the ovary from which the now fertilized egg was released and for the last six or seven months of pregnancy by the placenta, the mammary glands increase in size. The flow of milk is initiated by a hormone released by the pituitary gland.

The importance of the long period of development after birth has been stressed previously. Though a child's basic genetic make-up is inherited in the chromosomes contributed by its mother and father, its environment can affect full use being made of its genetic potential particularly in the first few years of its life.

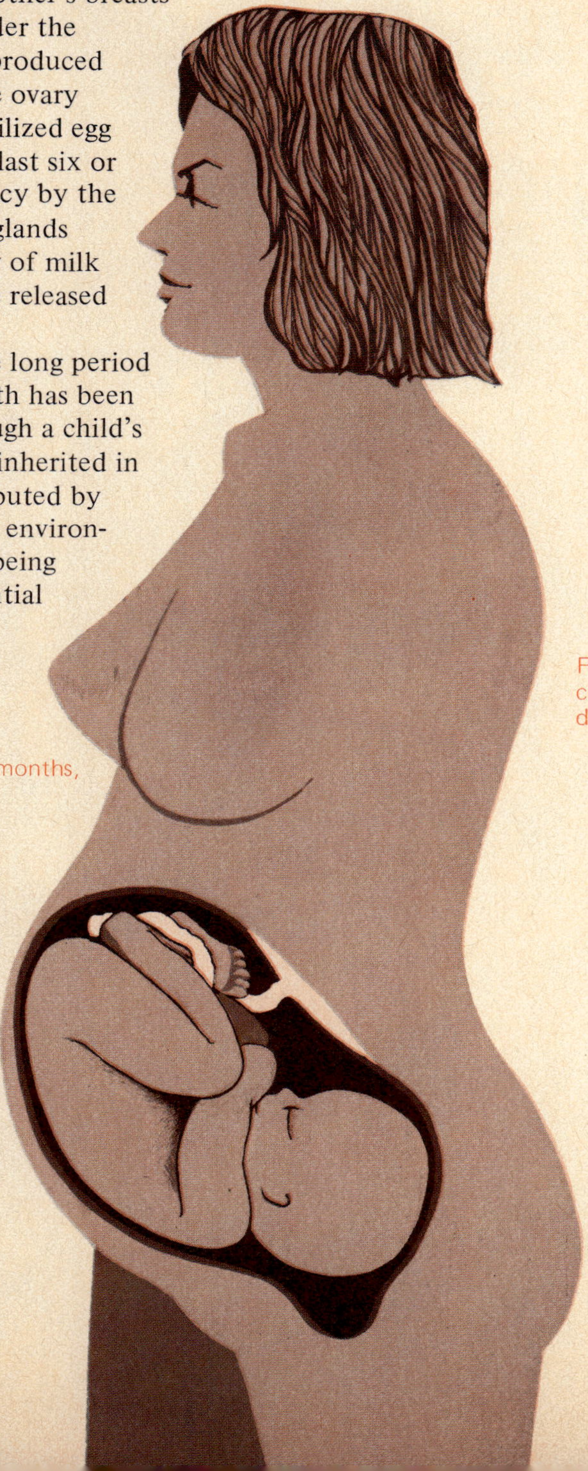

Fig 77. Full term baby at 9 months, ready to be born

Fig 78. Environment can have a considerable effect on a child's development

Problems
(A) Semen is filtered and the filtrate (containing no sperms) added to some frog's eggs. No tadpoles hatch from the eggs.
(B) Semen is filtered and the material held back (containing sperms) is added to the filtrate and then to the frog's eggs. Tadpoles eventually hatch from the eggs.
What conclusions would you make from these results?

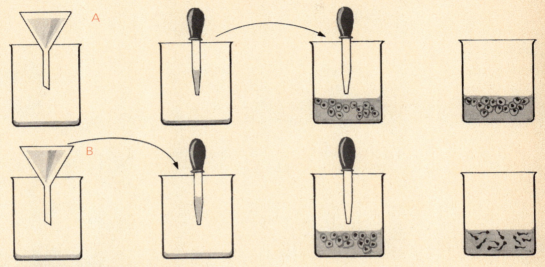

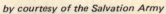
by courtesy of the Salvation Army

10 Cells and genetics

Cells and tissues

If you gently scrape the inside lining of your mouth with a teaspoon handle or something similar, you will obtain a creamy fluid. Place this on a glass slide and add a drop of water to it. Look at it under the low power of the microscope and draw what you see. What do the structures you obtained with the spoon indicate about the lining of the mouth? If you now add a drop of methylene blue or Delafield's haematoxylin to the fluid and leave it for a minute or so, what do you see under the microscope? What are you able to say about the reaction of different parts of the structures you see to either of the two stains?

When you scrape the inside of your mouth you remove some of the cells of the lining. Looking at each cell you are able to see the small darker area or *nucleus* surrounded by the clear *cytoplasm*. The stain helps you to see the nucleus more clearly for it is the only part of the cell that accepts the methylene blue or haematoxylin.

If you look at a joint of meat carefully you will notice that it is made up of different layers of tissue; tough, white bone with soft, red marrow in the middle; softer, glassy, flexible cartilage; red, fibrous muscle tissue; whitish fat which does not have fibres and which breaks up easily; thin, clear, tough connective tissue surrounding the muscles and separating the blocks of tissue; hollow tubes—the blood vessels, some containing blood; and probably white nerve fibres. If you examine pieces of liver or kidney you will see that these have a very different make-up compared with the fleshy joint of meat.

Each kind of tissue—liver, kidney, muscle, etc—has its own distinct appearance and properties. If you look at small pieces or slices of them under the microscope you will see that they are made of cells, just as the lining of your cheek is. Each is made up of different types of cells, and this accounts for the extraordinary differences between different organs. The illustrations show some of the many different kinds of cells and tissues.

Bryan Clarke

Fig 79. Cells from inside of cheek

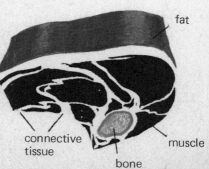

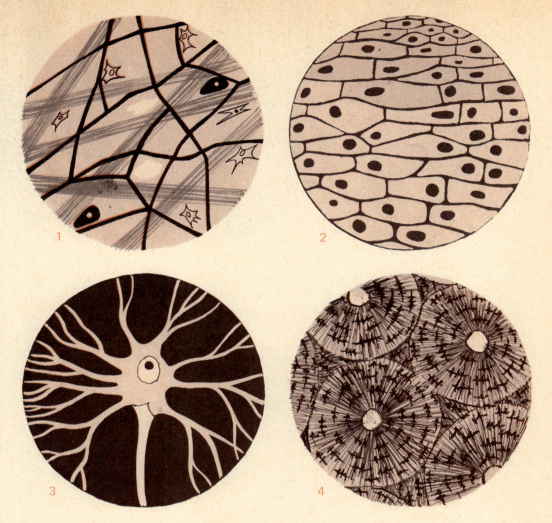

Fig 80. Different human cells and tissues

1 Areolar or loose connective tissue
2 Epithelium
3 Nerve tissue
4 Compact bone tissue

Cells under the microscope

Using the low power of the microscope you were able to see the *nucleus* and surrounding *cytoplasm* of the cheek lining cells. Staining the cells showed up the nucleus more clearly. Stains are chemicals, or mixtures of chemicals, that 'react' with chemical substances in part of the cell and make those parts easier to see. Some stains become attached only to certain parts (they are *specific*) and can be used, therefore, to identify particular types of cell or parts of cells.

By using special stains and techniques and higher magnifications of the microscope it has been possible to work out very fine structures in cells and to identify many of the chemicals present. All cells have *protoplasm* as their basis. Protoplasm is a complicated mixture of chemicals undergoing a great number of chemical changes, and its composition varies greatly from one species of living thing to another. It consists largely of *water* containing *proteins*, fatty substances *(lipids), carbohydrates* and *salts.* The drawing shows the structure of an animal cell that has been revealed using the electron microscope, a type of microscope that uses electrons (electrons help to produce the picture in a television tube) instead of light. You can see that within the protoplasm is a complicated system of canals and other structures. The contents of each cell are enclosed by a thin *cell membrane*—the outermost part of the living cell (less than $\frac{1}{1000}$ mm thick). Experiments indicate that this plays a part in regulating the movement of substances between a cell and neighbouring cells. The membrane is thought to consist of protein and lipid material. (In plants the cell wall is made of more rigid cellulose—a carbohydrate —see page 13).

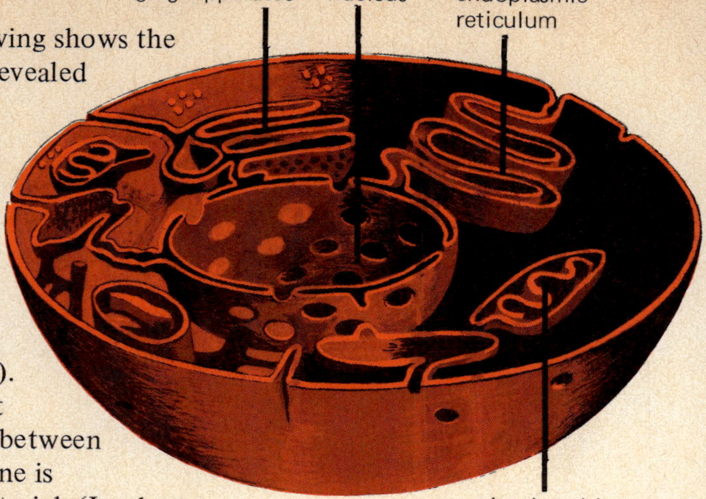

Fig 81. Diagram through an individual cell

The nucleus

This small structure controls all the changes that occur in each cell including its growth and composition. Within the protoplasm (*nucleoplasm*) of the nucleus are proteins called *nucleoproteins*. These important molecules regulate protein manufacture in the *cytoplasm, (the protoplasm surrounding the nucleus).* The nucleus itself is surrounded by a membrane similar to the cell membrane.

At certain times the denser material in the nucleus becomes more clearly visible as coiled threads, the *chromosomes.* In humans each cell in the body (except for egg and sperm cells) has 46 chromosomes, arranged in females in 23 pairs (in males there are 22 pairs and 2 odd chromosomes). Other animals (and plants) have different numbers (eg fruitflies 8 in 4 pairs).

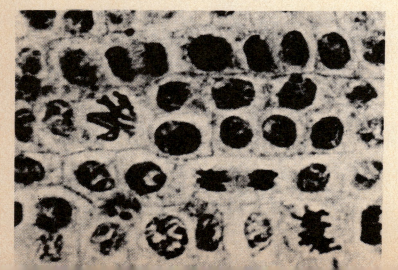

Fig 82. Cell division

Introducing Genetics

All the many different kinds of cells develop from an egg cell (*ovule*) which has fused with a sperm cell (see page 83).

If you look at, say, a sheep egg cell and that of a cow, there is no apparent difference, yet the cow egg will grow into all the different kinds of cells of the cow and the sheep egg into a sheep. Each tiny egg cell contains very little material, yet within this there must be sufficient differences to account for the fact that different animals are produced from egg cells which apparently look alike. But how do the egg cells differ and what decides how they develop in the way they do? Read the description of Mendel's experiments and the accounts of mitosis and meiosis that follow.

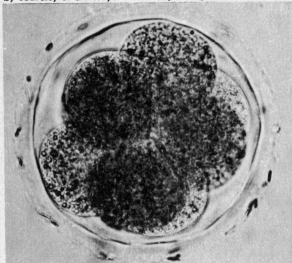

by courtesy of the Royal Veterinary College

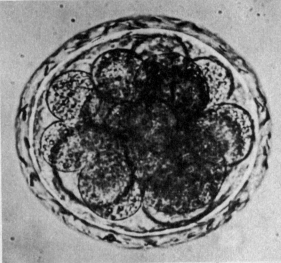

by courtesy of the Agricultural Research Council

Fig 83.
A. Sheep Ovum
B. Cow Ovum

Mendel's experiments

When a European monk Gregor Mendel conducted some experiments with pea plants around the middle of the nineteenth century chromosomes had not been discovered and it was not known how characteristics are passed on from one generation to the next. Mendel noted that amongst garden pea plants there were distinct differences, for instance, some plants were tall, some short, and some had wrinkled seeds, others round seeds. He decided to study these characters and selected plants with opposite characters (eg tall and short) and bred them until he got only tall plants from tall plant seeds, and short plants from short plant seeds, ie they were true-breeding or pure lines. Pea plants are self-pollinating, so Mendel had to make sure that self-pollination would not happen before he started his experiments. To do so he removed the stamens of the plants to be pollinated before they had ripened. He then transferred the pollen from the stamens of a tall plant to the stigma of a short plant whose stamens had been removed (A). He also put pollen from short plants on to the stigmas of tall plants (B).

When the resulting seeds ripened, he collected and planted them. Only tall plants resulted (C), (whatever it was that produced small plants seemed to have vanished), but when these tall plants were allowed to self-pollinate, some of the plants obtained from the seeds were tall and others were short (D). The shortness seemed to have reappeared. Mendel used thousands of plants and his results with large numbers of plants always showed a 3:1 ratio of tall to short plants from such crosses.

Now since seeds are produced from an ovule fertilized by a pollen grain, whatever it is that decides how a seed develops must be present in either the ovule or the pollen grains. Where the pollen was obtained from a tall plant and the ovule from a short plant, the resulting tall plant must have received its tallness from the pollen. Similarly an ovule from a tall plant must provide the tallness resulting from a cross with pollen from a short plant. The shortness has been over-ruled (E). But shortness must still be present for it to 'reappear' in a quarter of the offspring produced by self-pollinating the all tall first generation plants (C). Tallness and shortness must stay separate in some way. Tallness and shortness Mendel called 'factors'. Because tallness appears in preference to shortness when the two factors are present together, tallness is called the *dominant* factor and shortness the *recessive* factor.

If we allow tallness to be represented by T and shortness by t, the all tall parent plants would produce T sex cells, T in pollen and T in ovules. The short plants would have t pollen and t ovules. Either cross produced Tt first generation offspring. Now if the pollen and the ovules contained Tt the result of self-pollinating would be Tt Tt and the next generation would have sex cells with double the number of factors present. This obviously could not go on happening generation after generation. But if the pollen were either T or t, during a cross plants would be produced in the 3:1 ratio (F).

During the production of eggs and pollen cells do they receive only half of the instructions (factors) for height from their parent?

Some years after Mendel's experiments, it was discovered that sex cells have nuclei containing chromosomes, a fixed number for each species of living organism. When a cell divides, copies of the chromosomes must be made (see page 99) for the daughter cell to receive the same instructions. But

Fig 84. Mendel's experiment

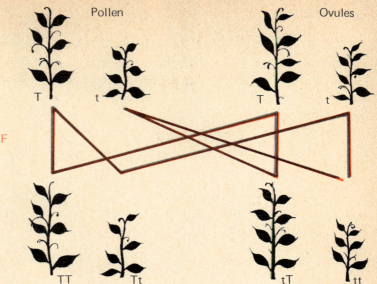

Fig 84. Mendel's experiments, 3:1 ratio

when sex cells are produced, if the number of chromosomes in offspring—formed by an egg cell joining with a sperm cell—is not to double, the chromosome number must be halved. During meiosis the human number of 46 is reduced to 23 so that human egg and sperm cells only have 23 chromosomes. This would seem to fit in with the evidence that if Tt (tallness and shortness) are present in the cells of first generation pea plants, the sex cells only have T or t. The factors or instructions would appear to behave like the chromosomes in meiosis. From this we believe that the chromosomes carry the instructions and these decide how the organism develops. Humans are extremely complicated creatures; and obviously with 23 pairs of chromosomes many opposing factors must be carried on each chromosome—each is a library of instructions.

Mendel's work enabled him to put forward two laws of inheritance. In the first, the *law of segregation*, he stated that *only one of a pair of opposite factors* (such as those for tallness and shortness, smoothness and roundness) *can be carried in a single cell* (that is, either tallness or shortness will be in, say, a pollen grain but not both). The second law—*the law of independent assortment* was that *each one of a pair of factors can combine with either one of another pair.* In other words, for example, a tall plant can produce either round or wrinkled peas; wrinkled peas may be green or yellow.

Parents and children

Mendel's factors we call *genes*. They can be regarded as packets of chemical information or chemical messengers which not only pass information from parents to their children but which provide the information controlling growth and all other processes. Each gene has a particular place on a chromosome and, since chromosomes occur in pairs in body cells, each gene has an opposite or partner on the other chromosome in the pair.

Although some gene pairs control individual traits most human features are the result of the action of several genes, as with hair colour, for instance. It is now known how many genes behave and what effect they produce and so it is possible to predict in many cases which characteristics children will inherit from their parents. This is becoming increasingly important with certain diseases, where it is known that a particular combination of genes or gene defects will produce the disease. If it is known beforehand that the parents have certain gene groupings then they can be advised not to have children should the probable defect be a serious one. Mongolism, for instance, is caused by an extra chomosome.

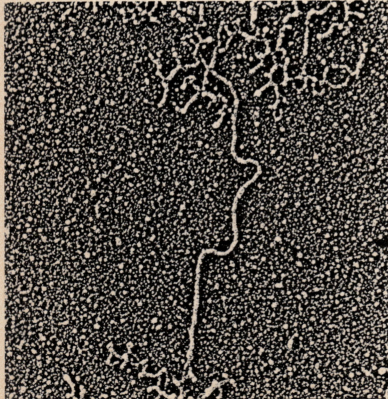

Fig 86. Single gene (the single strand in the centre) photographed under an electron microscope

by courtesy of IPS, USIS

You will remember that in women there are 23 pairs of chromosomes (the 23rd pair is known as XX). In men there are 22 pairs plus 2 odd chromosomes. Only half the XX pair is present together with an odd Y chromosome (a man has 22 pairs + X + Y). The X chromosome in men often carries genes other than those concerned with sex and the characters these produce are said to be *sex-linked*.

The gene producing red/green colour blindness (someone affected cannot distinguish between green and red), is an example, but fortunately it is recessive to the gene for normal vision so that a woman rarely has the defect. But it may be carried by the mother even though she is not colour blind and so it can be passed from her to her children. The Y chromosome has no gene for normal vision so that should the colour blindness gene be passed to a male he will be colour blind. A son will not receive the recessive gene from his father because only the Y chromosome will go to the son.

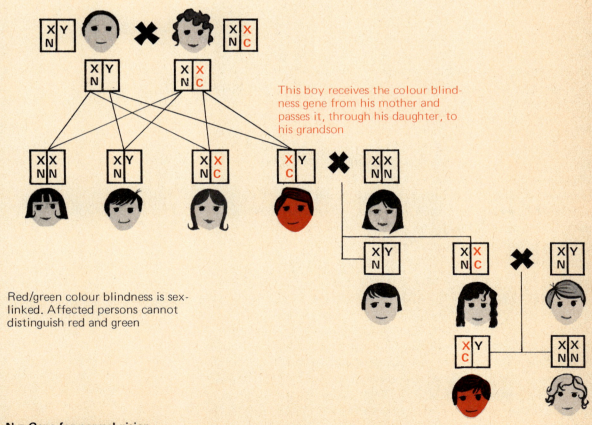

Fig 87. Diagram showing the inheritance of colour blindness

This boy receives the colour blindness gene from his mother and passes it, through his daughter, to his grandson

Red/green colour blindness is sex-linked. Affected persons cannot distinguish red and green

This boy is colour blind like his grandfather

N = Gene for normal vision
C = Gene for colour blindness
N is dominant and, when present, overrules the action of C.

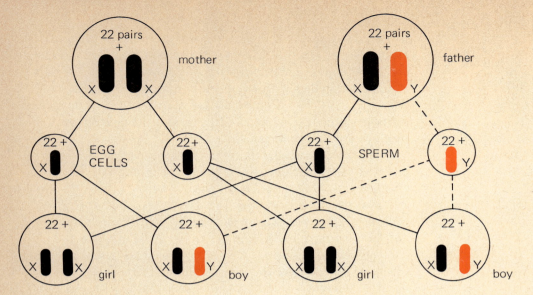

Fig 88. Diagram to show there are equal chances of girl or boy babies

Boy or girl?

Because the human male has 22 pairs + X + Y chromosomes, during the cell division producing sperm cells half of the sperm will receive X chromosomes and half will receive Y. Every egg cell of the female will contain X (from XX), so that when sperm cells fuse with egg cells there is an approximately equal chance of an X fusing with an X or a Y. If X fuses with X, a girl will result; X fusing with Y produces a boy.

Breeding plants and animals

For many hundreds of years man has been selecting and growing plants and animals, long before he understood the laws of inheritance or knew anything of Mendel's discoveries. He chose cereals and plants producing the largest seeds or most attractive flowers, the cattle producing most meat or milk, sheep producing the best wool and so on.

The earliest attempts to control plant fertilization were made early in the eighteenth century, when pollen was transferred artificially from one kind of carnation to another. By crossing plants in this way it meant that at least people were not relying on random pollination, but they were selecting plants with characters that they wanted and combining them to try and produce even better plants. Nowadays plant breeders practise very similar methods, but they know what the likely result will be and why. As a result we now have varieties of wheat which can grow and ripen in the short growing season of very northerly latitudes and which can survive cold temperatures. Varieties of cereals with very high resistance to certain plant diseases have also been produced.

CELLS AND GENETICS

Wheat

Barley

Oats

Fig 89. New varieties produced by plant breeding

by courtesy of the Plant Breeding Institute—Cambridge

Occasionally in nature certain chance combinations of genes or changes in genes (*mutations*) occur. Generally these produce a defect in the plant or animal, but a few are advantageous. Breeders will then select and breed from the new variety. Because mutations occur infrequently in nature, scientists expose plants to radiation which can cause changes in the chromosomes. The few improved varieties produced artificially in this way can be selected and used for breeding so that improved plants are produced more quickly than by waiting for nature to produce a favourable mutation. Plant breeding is a long term process. At least 10 years may be necessary for a successful new variety to be introduced. New strains have to be grown under a variety of conditions and compared with the parent strains for disease resistance, time taken to ripen, drought, cold or heat resistance and many other factors before they can be introduced commercially. If drought resistance, for example, can be improved only at the expense of yield it may be better to grow the heavier yielding variety and ensure that it is watered artificially during dry conditions.

Cell Reproduction

The cells of the body each have 46 chromosomes arranged in pairs (22 + 2 odd chromosomes in males, 23 pairs in females). When a cell divides into two the daughter cell produced must have the same chromosome content as the original cell if it is to act chemically like the original cell. During cell division (*mitosis*) copies of the chromosome pairs are made (see page 98) and so the daughter cell is formed with a complete set of chromosomes. You will remember that an embryo grows from a fertilized egg cell— an egg cell whose nucleus has fused with the nucleus of a sperm cell. Egg cells and sperm cells each have a nucleus containing chromosomes just as body cells do, but if an egg cell with 46 chromosomes joined with a sperm cell possessing 46 chromosomes the fertilized egg cell would contain 92 chromosomes as would all the cells formed from it. When this new individual reproduced, its chromosomes would double in number, and so on, obviously an impossible situation.

During the development of egg cells and sperm cells, therefore, a different kind of cell division occurs, called *meiosis*. In this the chromosome number is halved (see page 99) so that the sex cells have half the number of chromosomes of normal body cells. When a human egg cell nucleus fuses with a sperm cell nucleus, therefore, 23 chromosomes in the egg cell will join with 23 chromosomes from the sperm giving a fertilized egg cell with 46 chromosomes.

Mitosis

When a cell is not dividing the chromosomes cannot be seen using an ordinary light microscope. But when the nucleus starts to divide the chromosomes can be seen as double threads. They must make copies of themselves before visible changes happen.

Mitosis is, of course, a continuous process: the diagrams summarise the sequence of changes that take place. Each chromosome can be seen to consist of two threads. They become arranged around the equator of a spindle-shaped network of strands– the *spindle*. The two threads of each chromosome separate and pull apart towards the poles of the spindle. A nuclear membrane forms round each set of chromosomes and the cell divides into two.

All the changes take place within the cell membranes (not shown in the diagrams). A cell with 4 chromosomes is illustrated

Fig 90. Sequence showing mitosis

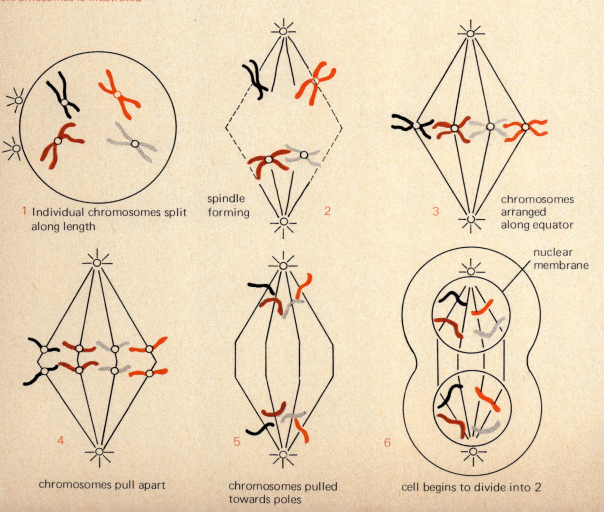

1 Individual chromosomes split along length

2 spindle forming

3 chromosomes arranged along equator

4 chromosomes pull apart

5 chromosomes pulled towards poles

6 cell begins to divide into 2 — nuclear membrane

Meiosis

When sex cells are formed the number of chromosomes is halved (this is called *meiosis*): each cell has half the number of chromosomes possessed by body cells. In the early stages of meiosis the chromosomes can be seen as *single* threads (*not* double as in mitosis). Meiosis, like mitosis, is a continuous process. The diagrams summarise the main events, with 6 chromosomes shown. The single thread chromosomes pair, forming three pairs, whose members then split. The split chromosomes pull apart remaining attached in one or two places, and the pairs become arranged on a spindle rather as in mitosis and the individual chromosomes move to the poles, each chromosome of each of three pairs pulling apart, resulting in two daughter cells each containing three split chromosomes—half of the six in the original cell. A second division similar to mitosis then follows resulting in the production of four sex cells, each with three chromosomes.

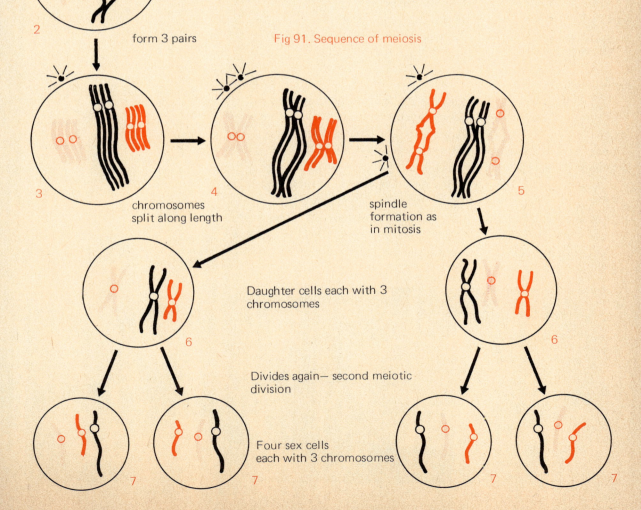

Fig 91. Sequence of meiosis

11 Disease causing organisms

The Black Death that swept through Europe in the 14th century is thought to have resulted in the death of 25,000,000 people—1 in 4 of the population—and the Great Plague of 1665 reduced London's population of just under half a million by a similar proportion. The plague causing organism—a rod-shaped bacterium—was discovered only in 1894, not long after Louis Pasteur, the great French scientist, had first shown that many diseases are caused by bacteria. Bacteria, viruses, protozoa (single celled animals) and many kinds of worms such as roundworms, flukes and tapeworms are organisms that cause diseases. A disease may be defined as any unhealthy condition of the body or part of it.

But not all diseases are due to organisms—many are the result of chemical or structural defects of an organ or tissue. Mental illness is the most common form of ill health.

Viruses

These minute organisms are on the borderline between the living and non-living, and, as more are discovered, we are becoming increasingly aware that they are important producers of disease. Common examples affecting man are those causing influenza, smallpox, poliomyelitis and the common cold. Viruses also cause diseases in animals and plants and those affecting domestic animals and plants are especially important. Foot and mouth disease affecting cattle and sheep is a virus infection, as is distemper in dogs. Potato leaf roll and tobacco mosaic diseases are examples of virus diseases of plants.

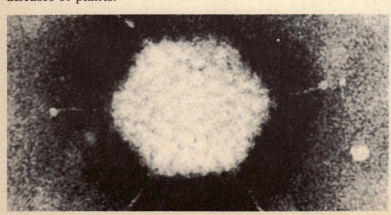
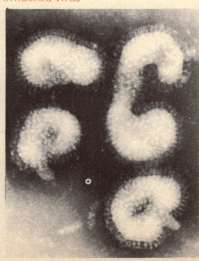

Fig 92. Photomicrographs of viruses—on the left an intact particle of Adenovirus type 5, on the right an influenza virus

DISEASE CAUSING ORGANISMS

The smallest viruses are about $\frac{1}{100\,000}$ mm ($\frac{1}{2\,500\,000}$ in) across and the largest only $\frac{\cdot 3}{10\,000}$ mm ($\frac{1}{80\,000}$ in)

Viruses are able to grow and increase in numbers only in a living cell and their activities may result in the death of the cell. In some way, not yet fully understood, the virus is able to insert itself into the cell's chemical machinery using this to grow and multiply.

Viruses are generally passed from one person to another by direct contact, in breathing, or sneezing and coughing. The yellow fever virus is transmitted by a mosquito when it pierces the human skin to suck up the blood on which it feeds. Some viruses, polio and influenza viruses for example, specifically affect certain tissues—nerve cells and the cells of the breathing system respectively.

Antibiotics (see page 106) are not directly effective against viruses though doctors do prescribe them as the body, weakened under virus attack, may be particularly susceptible to bacteria and other organisms.

Practical problems

1. Mix in a beaker 2ml freshly obtained loam and 10ml newly distilled water in a sterile beaker. Place a sterilized loop of platinum wire in the mixture and scrape it gently across a sterile culture medium in a petri dish. Place the petri dish in a warm oven and leave for a few days, looking at the medium each day. What do you observe?
Also set up controls with distilled water and thoroughly heated soil + distilled water only.
Why are the controls necessary and what do they show?
2. Place a fly under the cover of a petri dish containing sterile culture medium and allow it to walk over the surface. (Fig 93) Remove the fly and place the dish in an oven as in the previous experiments. What do you observe after leaving the dish for a few days as in the previous experiment?
What would you expect to happen if you placed the petri dish in a refrigerator instead of a warm oven?

To make a culture medium

Place 3·5gm of gelatine on 250ml of boiling water and stir until it dissolves. Then add 0·5gm of Marmite and 0·5gm of glucose. Boil until these have dissolved, then pour into three sterilized petri dishes.

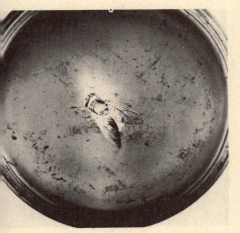

Fig 93. Petri dish with fly and a few days growth of virus and bacteria

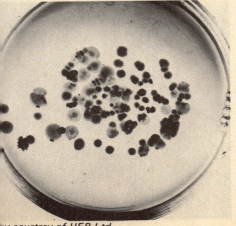

y courtesy of HEB Ltd.

Bacteria

These are tiny single-celled organisms usually classified as plants as they have a cellulose cell wall. They are able to extract material from their surroundings to make the energy required for living. There are many different kinds of which, fortunately, relatively few cause disease. In fact many are useful. Some live in the soil where they break down organic compounds into simple chemicals that plants can absorb through their roots. Certain bacteria are even used to make such products as cheese and vinegar. Those that cause disease of man are a serious problem, however. (Some cause diseases of plants and animals).

Disease causing bacteria are called *pathogens*. Examples are those producing boils, pneumonia, typhoid, tetanus and diphtheria. Many pathogens are unable to use inorganic substances from their surroundings to build up the substances required by living processes; they are totally reliant on ready made food substances already digested by their host. Most grow inside the body but some are able to reproduce by means of spores.

Those living in oxygen rich surroundings—eg the linings of the ear, mouth, nose, throat and lungs are said to be *aerobic*. Those living in the absence of free oxygen, in deep wounds for example, are *anaerobic*. The organisms causing tetanus and gas gangrene are *anaerobes*.

There are three main kinds of bacteria: (a) round or spherical ones called *cocci*, (2) rod-shaped *bacilli*, (3) spirally-shaped *spirilli*. The table (p.104) lists examples of each. Bacteria act in the body in two main ways (a) by destroying vital cells, (b) by releasing chemicals (*toxins*) that interfere with chemical processes.

They can be spread through sneezing and coughing, poor hygiene—such as not washing hands after using the toilet, unclean dustbins encouraging rats, flies and other pests, by direct contact with an infected person and by animals, especially insects such as flies which carry germs on their legs and mouthparts and deposit them in food when feeding.

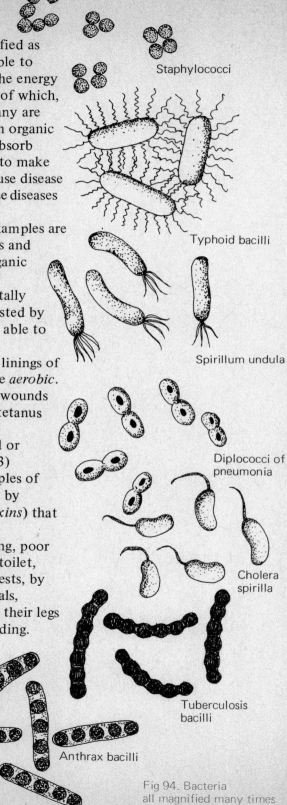

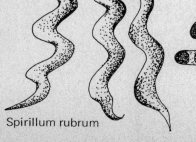

Fig 94. Bacteria all magnified many times

DISEASE CAUSING ORGANISMS 103

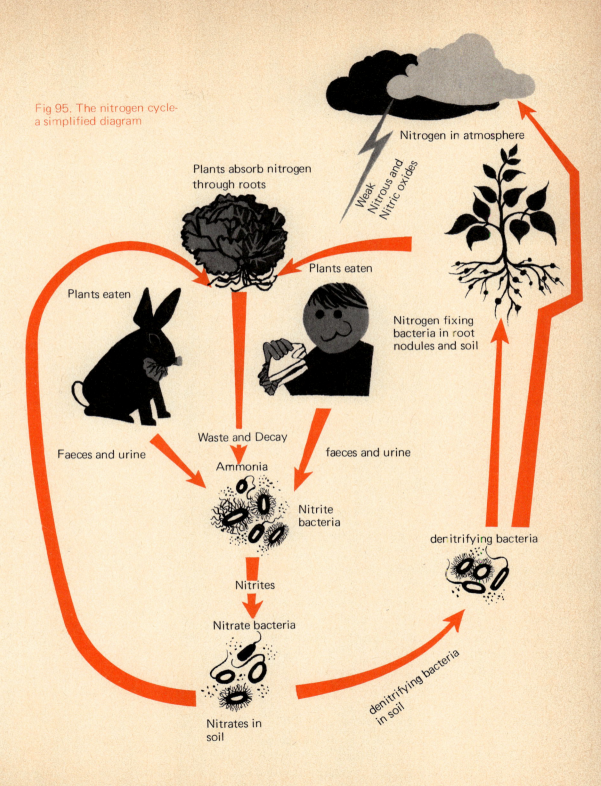

Fig 95. The nitrogen cycle - a simplified diagram

Disease causing bacteria

Organism	Disease
Cocci	
Staphylococcus	Boils
Streptococcus	Blood poisoning
Pneumococcus	Pneumonia
Bacilli	
Typhoid bacillus	Typhoid
Anthrax bacillus	Anthrax
Tetanus bacillus	Tetanus
Spirilli	
Relapsing fever spirillum	Relapsing fever
Syphilis spirillum	Syphilis

They enter the body through the skin—particularly as a result of insect or animal bites or through cuts, they may infect the hair roots, and through the linings of the nose, throat and lungs. Some bacteria live in parts of the body without causing disease but they grow and multiply in certain situations. Pneumonia diplococcus is harmless in the nose and throat, but if it multiplies in the lungs then it causes pneumonia. Some bacteria are specific—tuberculosis bacillus causes tuberculosis, the organism of diphtheria causes diphtheria but some diseases, eg pneumonia, can be produced by several different organisms.

Vaccination and immunity

The human body is continually attacked by disease producing organisms but its natural defences (*immunity*) are usually sufficient to overcome them. There are some bacteria and viruses that cause very unpleasant, even fatal diseases and it is possible to support the body's natural immunity through *vaccination*. Weakened or dead strains of the organisms concerned are prepared and injected or taken through the mouth. In the body they cause a mild reaction as though it were reacting to the disease itself and the antibodies added to the body's defences are available should a major attack follow at a later date.

Protection is available in this way against poliomyelitis, measles, whooping cough, diphtheria, and tetanus, for instance. Vaccines of the latter three are commonly injected into children before they start school as a three-in-one injection.

DISEASE CAUSING ORGANISMS 105

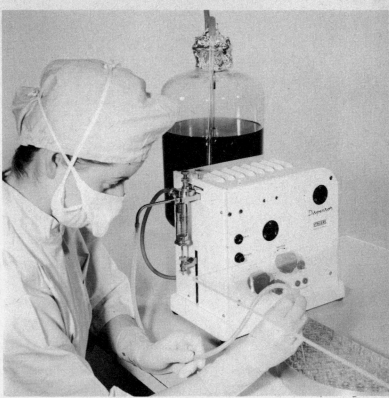

by courtesy of Glaxo Laboratories

Fig 96. Filling vials with measles vaccine

Fig 97. Taking a throat swab

Identifying bacteria

Many of the diseases caused by bacteria can be identified by the symptoms they produce. Measles and chicken pox, for example, usually have a characteristic rash. Often it is necessary to try to identify the organisms concerned so that doctors can prescribe the right form of treatment. This is the task of the bacteriologist. A sample of blood or a swab (see illustration) from the nose or throat may be taken to collect samples of the pathogens and in carefully controlled sterile (germ free) laboratory conditions they are cultured (grown) to help identify them. The bacteriologist uses various tests or factors:- size and shape; reaction to special stains; reaction to special substances that encourage or restrict growth; effect of heat and drying; and effect on laboratory animals.

Where an infectious disease is concerned, every effort must be made to limit its spread. Particular care has to be taken in hospitals. Soiled linen has to be sterilized by boiling and copious use made of disinfectants; all soiled dressings are burned in an incinerator. Conditions in hospital wards and operating theatres are kept as germ free (*aseptic*) as possible. All instruments, dressings, cloths, etc used in treatment are sterilized.

by courtesy of St Bartholomew's Hospital

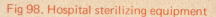
Fig 98. Hospital sterilizing equipment

Antibiotics

When a person does become ill from an infection and the organism responsible has been identified (or the symptoms recognised) a doctor usually prescribes drugs called *antibiotics*. These are so named because originally they were produced from living organisms, but nowadays some are manufactured synthetically by chemists. Some antibiotics attack certain germs only, others known as broad spectrum antibiotics are effective against a number of different germs.

The first attempts to produce drugs to combat particular bacteria were made by the German doctor, Paul Ehrlich (1854-1915). He found that some dyes could stain germs and not the tissues and he then attempted to link such a dye with a chemical germ destroyer. The 606th chemical tried was successful. Gehard Domegk developed Ehrlich's work and discovered *Prontosil*. Part of this substance, called *sulphanilamide*, was found to be effective on its own. It was the first of a whole range of synthetic drugs called sulphonamides. In 1928, however, Alexander Fleming discovered penicillin, a substance produced by the blue-green mould *Penicillium*. Like so many major discoveries it was made by chance. Fleming was culturing some moulds when he noticed that one of his samples had been contaminated by a fluffy piece of *Penicillium* mould. In an area surrounding

DISEASE CAUSING ORGANISMS 107

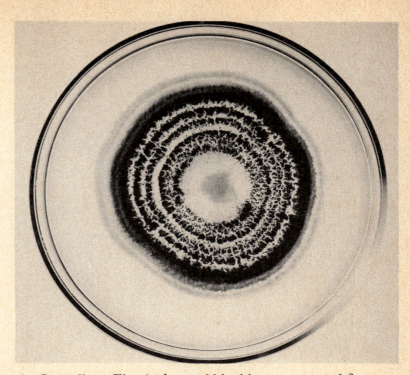

Fig 99. Penicillium mould

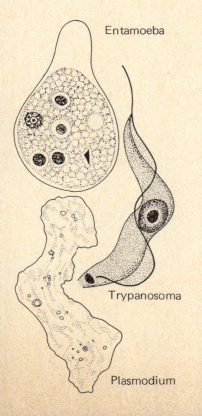

Fig 100. Disease—causing protozoa

the *Penicillium* Fleming's mould had been prevented from growing. Realising its significance, Fleming tried to extract the growth-preventing substances which the *Penicillium* must have been producing. But it was not until the late 1930's that a form of the substance named *penicillin* was prepared that could be injected. It became widely used during the second world war and many lives were saved. Many new forms have been developed since. A number of other antibiotics have been discovered following the development of pencillin for example, streptomycin and aureomycin, and there is a continuous search for others.

Protozoa

A number of these single celled animals cause illness in man. *Entamoeba*—related to *Amoeba*—causes dysentery (inflammation of the intestine). *Plasmodium* causes malaria, being passed into man's bloodstream by the bite of a mosquito. *Trypanosoma,* carried by the tsetse fly, causes sleeping sickness.

   Entamoeba spreads through poor hygiene, especially through people who handle food not washing their hands frequently enough, particularly after going to the toilet. When travelling to countries where malaria carrying mosquitoes occur, people are advised to use special protective drugs eg paludrine and when sleeping the use of mosquito nets is usual.

Worms

Many species of worms are parasitic in man, some causing serious illness, commonly in tropical and far-eastern countries. Roundworms, tapeworms and flukes are examples of parasitic worms.

The tapeworm (*Taenia*) is passed to humans in uncooked pork containing the bladder stage of the tapeworm's life cycle. Strict inspection of meat produced in and imported into Britain has eradicated tapeworm infections but in some foreign countries where inspection is less adequate they are still fairly common. It is important to thoroughly cook meat and fish to eliminate the danger of infection. The illustration shows the life cycle of the pork tapeworm.

Filaria, a roundworm, is carried by mosquitoes and spread to humans when the mosquitoes bite to suck blood. Like the *Trichina* worm it causes great damage to the tissues.

Schistosoma is a fluke causing serious illness in many tropical countries. The young stages live in water, and, if they come into contact with the bare skin, they bore through until they reach a blood vessel.

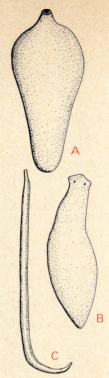

Fig 102. A—Trichina B—Schistosoma C—Renduram

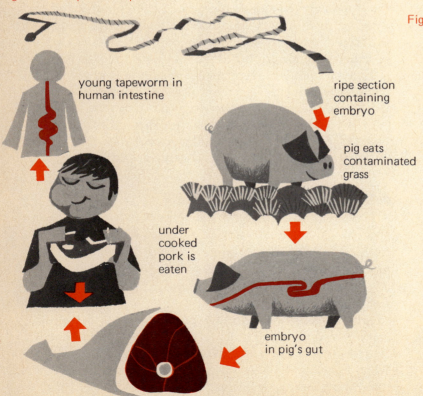

Fig 101. Lifecycle of Tapeworm

Mites

Mites are relatively unimportant as disease causing organisms. One living in the skin causes scabies, a very irritating skin rash. Another has recently been shown to cause asthma in some people. It lives in the dust on bed clothes, hence the importance of regularly changing and cleaning bed linen.

Fungi

Few fungi cause disease in man. Perhaps the best known is ringworm, so called becuase it often produces ring-shaped wounds in the skin.

Insects

These are well known pests of man and his domestic animals and plants. Lice, fleas, and 'bugs' of various kinds are the best known examples affecting man directly. Fleas, apart from causing direct irritation of the skin, can carry pathogenic bacteria which are passed to us when the fleas bite. Bubonic plague organisms, for instance, are carried by rat fleas. Bed bugs are still found in some poor districts. They emerge at night from their hiding places in cracks to feed on the blood of their sleeping hosts. Mosquitoes have been mentioned previously as carriers of organisms responsible for malaria and yellow fever. Other insects pass on typhus bacteria and many other disease causing organisms.

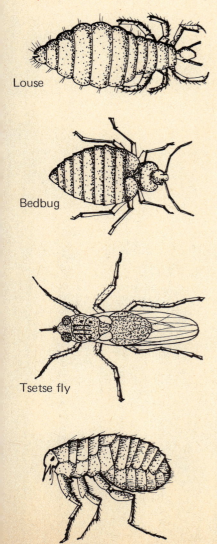

Fig 103. Disease transmitting insect pests

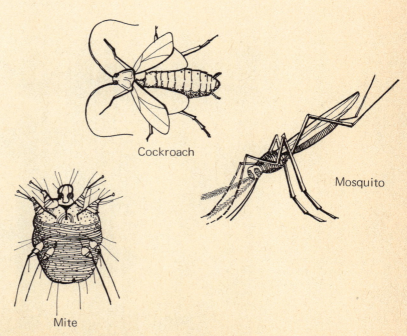

12 The community and its services

Controlling epidemic disease

The Black Death and the Great Plague have been mentioned previously as terrible epidemics of the past. At such times many futile attempts were made to control the disease, from burning wood with a strong smell to the wearing of lucky charms. With the discovery of so many bacteria from the 19th century onwards, and an understanding of their life cycles and the way in which they spread, it became possible to start trying to discover ways of controlling outbreaks of infectious diseases based on sound scientific principles instead of superstition.

The discovery for instance that rats carried the organisms responsible for bubonic plague meant that a war to exterminate as many rats as possible could be waged. Similarly, steps to remove fleas by ensuring personal hygiene helped reduce the number of outbreaks. Typhus, spread by bacteria carried by lice, has also been reduced through improved cleanliness and by destroying the carrier insects with insecticides.

Fig. 104.
The Black Death
(Gaigiullo D.)

by courtesy of the Mansell collection

The organisms causing cholera and typhoid were found to be carried in water or food. Public authorities now regularly inspect water and food supplies so that outbreaks of these diseases occur rarely in Britain and then only amongst immigrants or holiday makers returning from tropical countries where the standards of cleanliness are less good.

When an epidemic does occur every effort is made to isolate the people infected and to cure them by available drugs. All people who have come into contact with the disease must be traced and checked to see if they are infected. Rapid vaccination may have to take place to control any possible disease spread and public authorities of various kinds check all the possible sources of infection—food shops, water supplies and so on. Epidemics do tend to recur from time to time as with certain forms of influenza. Asian flu is an example; there have been several world-wide epidemics in recent years. Influenza is caused by certain kinds of virus but, although vaccines are available, mass vaccination of everyone is not really practical because each epidemic tends to be due to a different strain of virus. Limited vaccination is still possible however, from hastily prepared new vaccines, and this does prove effective in helping to control Asian flu epidemics, particularly as far as protecting weaker individuals—those suffering from asthma, bronchitis and other chest conditions—is concerned.

Fig 105.
Emergency vaccination in Uganda

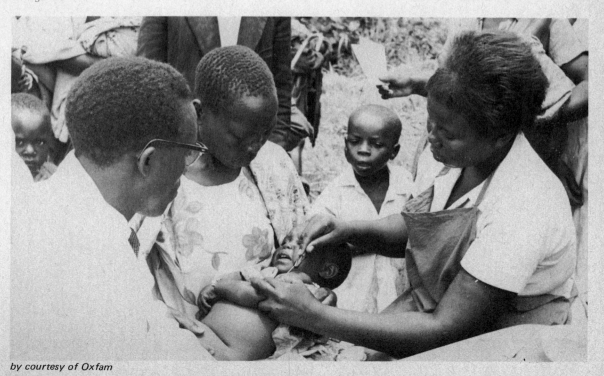

by courtesy of Oxfam

The supply of water

Not very long ago there was no public water supply—people drew water from a well bored in their garden or backyard and many shared such facilities. Today we take it for granted that at the turn of a tap we can obtain all the water we need. In a large town more than fifty gallons a day are supplied to each member of the population. Baths, showers, washing machines, car and garden hoses, hairsprays and other devices consume large quantities of water.

The law requires water companies to provide water that is not harmful to health or unsuitable for industrial processes, should not contain any visible particles of matter and it should not taste or smell. Most of the water supplied in Britain is obtained from rivers, but some towns are some distance from sufficiently large rivers and water then has to be piped to the local water works. Valleys are often dammed to produce artificial storage lakes. Manchester for instance, receives its water from such a 'drowned' valley in Westmorland.

Taken from rivers the water is pumped into large open reservoirs in which the purification process starts, for substances in suspension have time to settle and most of the pathogens die. Before the water can be passed through the water mains to homes it has to be filtered to remove unwanted matter—the first filters consist of coarse sand and the second of gravel covered with a layer of fine sand. The organic substances are broken down by the action of bacteria. Chemical treatment of the water may then be

Fig 106. Diagram of plan of town's water supply

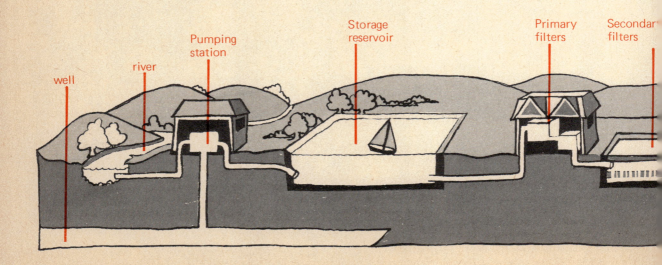

THE COUNTRY AND ITS SERVICES 113

by courtesy of Elan Valley Waterworks

Fig 107. The Gibson Dam in Breconshire, Wales

necessary to remove local impurities, after which, in the chlorination plant, chlorine gas (as used to purify water in swimming pools) is used to kill off harmful bacteria. Samples are tested for bacteria each day to make sure that the water is of the required standard of purity. It is stored in covered underground storage reservoirs and can then be pumped through the water mains for use in our homes and factories.

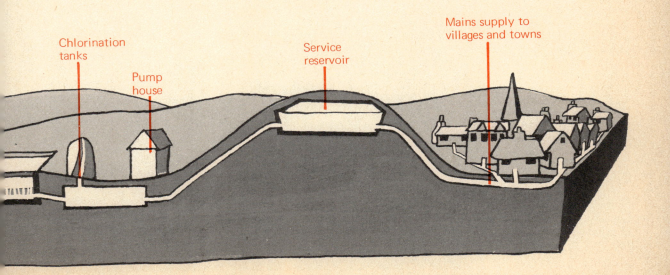

Refuse collection and disposal

The problem of refuse disposal is a continually growing one as more and more goods are produced in containers that have to be thrown away. The increased use of plastics is a particular worry for these are not easily dealt with. Tin cans can be extracted from garbage and the metal reused, and glass bottles, textiles and paper salvaged.

Each household produces on an average, a quarter of a hundred weight of rubbish every week, and obviously if this were not removed to special tips or collection points then its accumulation would be a health hazard, with flies, rats and other disease carrying animals attracted to it. Strikes of dustmen in London and New York have shown this recently.

Usually each local government authority is responsible for the collection of industrial and household refuse and its hygienic disposal. Great care must be taken to ensure that rubbish is not allowed to contaminate water supplies. Refuse is commonly tipped into disused quarries and used in the reclamation of low lying or marshy ground. But whereas at one time all rubbish was automatically dumped or thrown

Fig 108.
Britain's biggest incinerator at Edmonton. It deals with rubbish from eight London boroughs and nothing is wasted from the refuse. Heat from the furnaces is converted into electricity, metal is baled and sold for scrap and the clinker is sold for building and land drainage

by courtesy of the GLC

Fig 109. Diagram of plan of sewage-disposal plant

away, it has been realised that many items are recoverable and much of the remains can be converted into such useful materials as compost, even fertilizers. Cleansing departments are also responsible for street cleaning, removing dust, waste paper, etc and regularly emptying drain traps of the leaves and other materials that collect there.

Sewage disposal

Sewage consists of the waste matter from toilets, sinks, baths and from industry. It is collected by a system of drains which connect the large main drains—the *sewers*. These convey the sewage to the sewage works. Here the sewage is treated to remove solid materials and to render it safe before it is pumped into a river. The diagrams show a typical sewage works and summarise the changes that take place.

Sludge (a thick muddy liquid) is settled off from the rest of the sewage. It may be 'digested' by bacteria so producing valuable methane gas or it may be dried and used as a soil conditioner and fertilizer.

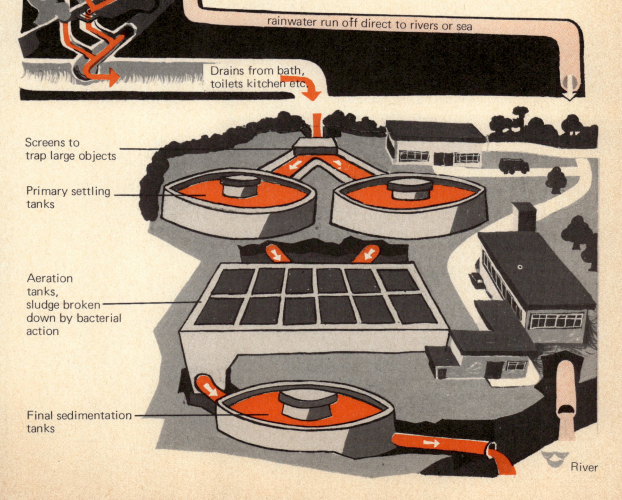

Air pollution

In a typical British town up to 300 tons of dirt and smoke particles fall on each square mile per year. Industrial and and domestic chimneys, motor vehicles, and other devices and processes release gases, dust, smoke and harmful contaminants into the air. These may help to cause fogs and have a serious effect on people's health, particularly those suffering from bronchitis and similar chest complaints. They make buildings dirty and cause considerable corrosion; the acids in the pollution eat away stonework, harming paintwork and other building surfaces. Dust in the air also helps to reduce the amount of sunshine reaching the ground. Sunshine is an important requirement for good health. Up to half the natural light may be lost by really bad air pollution. In the past when there was no control of air pollution, large cities such as London were notorious for their winter smogs—really bad fogs in which large amounts of dust, soot, sulphur and other pollutants are present. The Clean Air Act of 1956 aimed to reduce air pollution in cities by allowing local authorities to create so called 'smokeless zones'—areas where householders are not allowed to burn fuels that create smoke. Factories and other installations also were not allowed to or were restricted in their output of dark smoke. The Act has resulted in the production of special smokeless fuels for open fires and solid fuel boilers, and gas and electricity have become increasingly popular forms of heating.

Power stations are built with very tall chimneys to release any dust that is produced high into the atmosphere. The amount of dust in the air is regularly checked. There have been large reductions in the number of airborne particles in London and other large towns, but the growth in the number of motor cars has resulted in a great increase in the quantities of exhaust gases, including carbon monoxide. Very high levels have been recorded in the blood of some people, such as policemen on point duty, who spend a great deal of their time in conditions where traffic is heavy. Experiments have been carried out to try to reduce the quantities of harmful gases released, and also to make electric vehicles which release no waste products at all. In some parts of America laws have been introduced to restrict the emission of pollutants from car exhaust systems.

Town planning and urban development

In the past towns have grown haphazardly—without planning. At one time traffic largely consisted of people on foot with a few horse-drawn vehicles. The streets were narrow and uneven, without any proper drainage; sanitation and water supplies were non-existent and rubbish was allowed to accumulate, perhaps to be washed away with the next rainstorm. The closeness of the houses and the lack of hygiene resulted in epidemics spreading quickly.

Until recently the development of property has often been unregulated with the result that houses and factories have been mixed unwisely, open spaces have been inadequate or badly placed, and streets have not been planned and constructed to cope with the varying requirements of through and local traffic.

Widespread war damage in many large towns gave the opportunity to a number of local authorities for building and planning on a large scale, as has the growth of new towns and the general movement of people out from town centres. It

Fig 110. New town

Angela Phillips

was appreciated that although many properties were privately owned the overall appearance and planning of new developments were a public matter, with the result that many town and country planning departments have been established in the last few years.

Planning authorities have power to regulate the construction and design of buildings, to control the use to which they are put and their later development. Often particular areas of a town will be allocated for housing, for shops, for factories or for open spaces. In addition to developing new land, a local authority has a duty to ensure that slum areas where housing conditions are especially bad and likely to cause ill health are redeveloped. The authority can make a slum area a *clearance area* and after giving the owners due notice (during which they can appeal to various higher bodies) it can compel the owners to demolish the slums or it may itself buy the land and pull the buildings

Fig 111.
Slum clearance

by courtesy of John F White Studios

down. Alternatively, the area may be classed a *redevelopment area* rather than a clearance area and plans for redeveloping the area are submitted to the Ministry. The owners, too, may prepare redevelopment schemes to be submitted to the local authority. If approved the owners then redevelop the area.

Local authorities must ensure that houses are not overcrowded and help to avoid overcrowding by providing sufficient new homes. They are also required to class any property as fit or unfit for people to live in and they must ensure that any repairs are done necessary to make a house habitable. Often grants are made available to owners of older properties to enable them to carry out improvements such as installing bathrooms and internal toilets.

When a new town is planned or major redevelopment is to take place in an existing one, all the various departments or bodies concerned with the many services necessary that help in the efficient running of a town have to work very closely together to plan for the needs of an increased or changed population. The people who are to live in a new town need work so that a certain number of factories and other places of work must be provided.

Workers and their families need houses to which gas, water and electricity supplies have to be connected. Households and factories produce waste, which is disposed of by refuse collection services. The cleansing departments concerned need to know how many houses they will have to cope with and whether the houses have solid fuel heating or some other fuel source—this can affect the content of refuse and the equipment needed to deal with it. Liquid waste and rain water passes into the sewage system for purification before it is passed into our rivers. Schools have to be provided along with colleges for further education; hospitals, libraries, sports facilities, shops and many other amenities have to be provided.

People, their work and leisure activities create traffic which requires roads to carry local vehicles and those passing through. Adequate rail services and other means of communication may be necessary. The problem of coordinating all these various requirements is the task of the planning department. In providing for people's needs the planners also aim to produce an environment that is enjoyable to live in.

Of course unlimited money is not available and this ultimately is what limits the planner's scope. After the second world war authorities in Britain were slow to appreciate that so many people would be able to afford cars and that there would be a shift of passenger traffic from the railways to the roads as a result. Construction of motorways in Britain has lagged seriously behind North America and Europe, lack of money being the major factor in the present restriction on road-building. This has resulted in widespread congestion in town centres and on some main roads, particularly on routes leading to seaside resorts, motor racing circuits and similar places attracting large volumes of traffic.

Motor vehicles produce great amounts of exhaust gases which are important causes of pollution, a major health worry at the present time (see page 116). The scope for town and country planning departments is great therefore, as they attempt to solve the many outstanding problems affecting our surroundings and try to plan for the conditions expected in the future.

Fig 112. Traffic congestion

by courtesy of the Automobile Association